"Lucy's brave struggle to reclaim her life from an eating disorder provides a graphic yet poetic insight into the pain and suffering experienced by sufferers of eating disorders and will no doubt provide a positive incentive to others—both to those already in treatment and to those who are struggling to take that first step."

— Claire Vickery, CEO and founder of The Butterfly Foundation

"In her raw and compelling account of the experience of anorexia nervosa, Lucy strips away all grandiosity and pretension. Her cautious, tentative steps towards recovery should inspire not only those currently trapped by the illness or its relapses, but also families who all too often have their deep trauma minimized or trivialized."

— Amanda Jordan, chief executive officer of The Eating Disorders Foundation

"An intense and compelling insight into the mind of an anorexic. A must for family and friends."

— Rachael Oakes-Ash, author of *Good Girls Do Swallow* and *Anything She Can Do I Can Do Better*

BITING
ANOREXIA

A Firsthand Account of an Internal War

LUCY HOWARD-TAYLOR

New Harbinger Publications, Inc.

Publisher's Note

This publication is designed to provide accurate and authoritative information in regard to the subject matter covered. It is sold with the understanding that the publisher is not engaged in rendering psychological, financial, legal, or other professional services. If expert assistance or counseling is needed, the services of a competent professional should be sought.

Distributed in Canada by Raincoast Books

Originally published in Australia and New Zealand as *Biting Anorexia: A first-hand account of an internal war* by Finch Publishing Pty Limited, Sydney, Australia © Lucy Howard-Taylor, 2008

Copyright © 2009 by Lucy Howard-Taylor
          New Harbinger Publications, Inc.
          5674 Shattuck Avenue
          Oakland, CA 94609
          www.newharbinger.com

Cover design by Sara Christian
Cover image by Zubin Shroff/Stone/GettyImages
Text design by Amy Shoup and Michele Waters-Kermes
Acquired by Catharine Sutker
Edited by Brady Kahn

Library of Congress Cataloging in Publication Data on file

Printed in the United States of America

11   10   09

10 9 8 7 6 5 4 3 2 1

First printing

CONTENTS

AUTHOR NOTE

I have purposely omitted specific weights throughout this book, preferring to refer to them as "-kilograms." Firstly, because I find them triggering, secondly because those with a similar predisposition to self-implosion may too, and thirdly, because the weight is merely emblematic of the problem. It is not the problem itself.

Names have been abbreviated to first initials to protect the privacy of individuals.

FOREWORD

I first met Lucy over the Internet on a "pro-ana" website. We had a lot in common. We were both in the grip of anorexia. We were both the same height.

Two years ago, she and I were the same weight for a period of time. We would send each other photos of our damaged and starved bodies. And in these photos Lucy wasn't fat. She was skinny. And I could see it...anyone could see it...*but she couldn't see it*. And she was the same weight as me.

When this eventually dawned on me, I said to her, "Lucy, we're the same. We're the same weight and height. I might be ten years older but I'm still the same size..." and if she could look at my photos and tell me that I wasn't fat, then she mustn't be fat either. And vice versa.

That's really how my recovery started. That's how I held onto this thought that I wasn't really the huge blimp I thought I saw when I looked in the mirror. I wasn't going to get to see it. You don't get to see it when you're starved with becoming as thin as possible...but I could see it on other people. I could see it on Lucy. If I could spend my time encouraging people like Lucy to get better, maybe it would make it easier for me to see it on myself.

I didn't belong on a "pro-ana" forum. None of us did, perhaps... but it's where we met. It's where we became friends. I started *We Bite Back* (www.webiteback.com) soon after realizing that if I spent my time encouraging other people to accept themselves as they were, eventually I would become more at ease with myself. The experience would "normalize" recovery for me, in the same way that being on pro-anorexic forums for years had normalized the emaciated form.

There are millions of people starving themselves right now in an effort to make themselves somehow acceptable. If one in four people is on a diet at any given time, then that is a lot of people overall who are unhappy with how they look. That's a lot of people who think the thinnest person in the room gets all the attention, success, relationships, and happiness. That's a lot of fixating on a distraction instead of putting our energies toward being the best people we can be.

There's this real temptation to reduce life to mere numbers. It isn't about numbers. I was so surprised when I read Lucy's book and found no mention of the numbers that she used to live and breathe by. Numbers are a distraction. *It's never really about food and weight.*

Everything changed for me in the months after creating *We Bite Back*. It was my own personal way of making recovery real for myself. Lucy was there on my new site from day one. She was one of the people I picked for my moderator team. Being an artist, I called my moderators the "post-mod squad." I figured we're trying to post-modernize online the eating disorder community by challenging the narrative that existed in pro-anorexic communities, places we had just left behind. In the end, we would come out of the thing as "post-pro-ana" or "post-ana." We would maintain some of the friendships we made even when we were sick and self-destructing, but we would move beyond the self-destruction itself. We would form friendships that weren't dependent on us remaining sick.

When you decide you're going to better yourself and spend each day trying to make a difference, your priorities shift around. When you go from being a reclusive homebody to someone who tries to positively engage others in your community, you start taking part in what's going on around you again. When you venture out to make friends again, it's uncomfortable and scary at first, but it gets easier.

This book is Lucy's story of her journey out of her eating disorder and fumbling into recovery, and finally coming out on the other side. *So thank you, Lucy.* Thank you for the brave poetic words you fed us when we were struggling in our darker moments. Thanks for the strong, jubilant words you wrote on *We Bite Back* as you embraced recovery and made it real for yourself.

Thank you Lucy, for believing in yourself. *Thank you for believing in me*. Thank you for being a positive role model. If everyone chose to recover so that it would help inspire others to take care of themselves, imagine the ripples it would cause in our social communities... I'm waiting for this to happen.

I think a lot of us are.

—Sharon Hodgson
Founder of *We Bite Back*
www.webiteback.com

ACKNOWLEDGMENTS

As insufficient as "thank you" seems, I want to first and foremost thank my mum and my dad, with everything I have, for unreservedly supporting me at every turn, and for your boundless love and sacrifice. "I love you" also seems insufficient, but as language fails to provide anything less than clichés for the heart, it will have to do. I want to thank my brother for putting up with me when I was narky or disparaging: I love you more than I can say, and I'm sorry I haven't said it more often. I want to thank my "Orange girls"—you beautiful, beautiful women of the world who deserve nothing less than the love of yourselves—you have inspired me, and buoyed me, and kept me writing. To my muse, for being my mirror. To my wonderful friends in real time, who have persuaded me to be faithful to myself, and who I feel thankful for every day—thank you. Your letter, Kate, stopped my free fall. The hours and hours we spent on the phone, Amelia, kept me upright. And to Jeremy, so endlessly patient, thank you for loving me and helping me to find the way to love myself. Margaret, thank you for the work that you do and for making me understand that I am as worthy of care and health as anyone else. Also to Sue and to Helen, for your support and help, and finally to Rex, Sam, and Carol, for taking me as I am and this book under your wing—without your dedication, this little bundle would not exist. Thank you.

White Mask

We light on each other, perhaps:
One into and over above –
flick! – we outrun
ourselves
and our Ophelias (shy pale and trembling).
The pot boils empty,
and we retreat to the edges
further together over paths recalled
(from last time?) –
tripping –
the strings sing as she does:
off tune.

PREAMBLE

To go forward, sometimes you have to go back

My name is Lucy Howard-Taylor. I am eighteen years old. I have starved myself silent. I have slipped through people and out of sight, into black. Rigid at night from fear, curled against another day, I fell: unmoved by the landing.

But this is not the exposé of an individual. This is a chronicle. Of anorexia. Of depression. Of you and me, perhaps. And a stumble back into the light.

Certainly, experiences as I have felt and held them center this book. This "memoir"? Perhaps, more appropriately, this "social commentary."

I am appealing to those of you who will feel this book, not just read it. I am appealing to your parents, to your family, your peers and colleagues, your judges. I am appealing to a social mockery and a stereotype that laughs off psychological torment as "selfish" and "vain."

My full name is Lucy Shena Howard-Taylor. I say it with a swing: Lu-cee Shee-naa How-erd-Tay-la. The "Lucy" was as unusual then as it is common now. The "Shena" is a combination of my grandmothers' names: Sheila and Una. People have always screwed up their faces and said "Wo-ow." I've come to think it's rather pretty.

I was considered "weird" all through school; now, at university, I am considered "eccentric." Which doesn't mean that I'm any less weird but merely that their vocabulary is getting better. I am a kooky, beatnik, artsy type. Apparently.

These are the things I like:

- The smell of an old and well-thumbed book.

- A fat cat who squawks and sits on my feet and another who sashays under my newspaper and misses the bench when she jumps.

- Subversive humor that feels really unfortunate.

- Halloumi cheese that squeaks and has been cooked crisp.

- Off-white grainy paper and scribbling with nicely blunted lead pencils.

- Businesspeople in the rain.

- Sydney University sandstone in the sun or winter or morning or rain.

- Nice peaky grass, soymilk (in hot chocolate), pepper-mint tea.

- Interesting people with a) an imagination, b) strange buttons, c) a brain (*whoa*), or d) a façade I can crack.

- Poetry of various persuasions and those arresting images one chances upon occasionally that make you lob your head to the side or the back with their seeming irrel-evancy yet startling truth.

- The Thesaurus, words and language.

- Oblivion (constant state of).

- Smiling at people who take it as a personal offense (see "businesspeople").

- Contemplating the enormous insignificance of all *this*.

I also have a particular fondness for puddles, blueberry bagels, and earrings with bits on them (I just bought a fantastic pair of mahjong earrings).

Of course, three years ago I was your "average" anorectic cradling myself in bed and wobbling against a tide of lettuce jokes and purging gaffes, who felt herself to be a social failure; a personal "nothing"; a waste of (too much) space. She who thought too much, who pushed too far and forgot to take a breather, who forced and forced herself through squares she really didn't fit, who withered with the agony of just not being "enough," just not being "right," and at the same time for just being "too much."

Back then I had too many thoughts and pain and responsibilities and expectation and *being...* I felt there was just too much "me" in relation to "them": the faceless them, the society of acceptables.

I am in recovery from anorexia nervosa, major depression, self-injury, and bulimia. It is still difficult for me to say this aloud. The social taboos surrounding these mental illnesses are just as vicious as they ever were. Mental illnesses are still seen as weaknesses of willpower or as a defect of personality. The depressed should "just snap out of it." The anorectics should just "open their mouths and chew." The fact that what we are dealing with is not so simple, but instead horribly complicated, is mostly bypassed.

I write this not to blame, but to challenge a society that all too commonly shrugs off the difficult and all too commonly ignores the ugly reflection of itself.

I have just turned eighteen as I write this. I should be writing an essay on the accuracy of Virginia Woolf's representation of women in interwar Britain. Clearly I am not, and that is both partly the result of procrastination and partly because I am trying not to think too much about the roasted hazelnuts I just gave my body. But mostly it is because I have something to say.

Here are the facts. Make of them what you will, but they are an attempt to establish a context for the barrage of self-hate I heaped upon myself for an indeterminate number of years. Here are memories; here are thoughts; here are parts of my past that psychiatrists have narrowed their eyes at and scribbled about on institutionally lined paper.

I was born in 1988 in Auckland, New Zealand, to two of the most wonderful people in the world. My dear little brother followed two years later.

My only memories of preschool involve food (lemon icy poles, Nutella, and extolling my own magnificence in being able to spread margarine), shyness (being unable to say one word to the poor boy I dubbed my "boyfriend," not being able to play musical chairs because I was terrified of dancing in public), and embarrassment (chiefly represented by one visual memory: a rearing pink bike manned by a blonde rival, cutting a corner and bearing down on my little, and very humbled, self, who mumbled tearfully and through a flush of red that she didn't know how to ride a bike—even with training wheels).

I was cocooned away in a private girls' school for twelve years. I was considered "precocious," a "prima donna," a "drama queen." In year 2, my teacher called me a "show-off." I invented wild personalities and lied chronically. One week I was Polynesian, the next I was supposed to be in a wheelchair, the next I was secretly an angel who could control the winds. I threw myself into imaginary universes, writing endless letters to nonexistent people and taking an invisible Anne (of Green Gables) to school with me. I lied to impress and confessed to assuage guilt. I lost friends as quickly as I made them with my propensity to overdramatize everything.

"There's nothing I quite so much enjoy," I remember saying, *"as a good argument and playground drama."* Needless to say, others did not feel similarly.

Time frustrated me. I was too young and there was too much to do. I was going to be an Oscar-winning actress. I was also going to be the first woman *president* of Australia. At the age of ten, I was endlessly frustrated at my inability to do anything "proper" and to have people take me seriously.

I remember lying in bed sick and being inspected by my mother and her friend. *"Goodness, she's got such big eyes!"* she said. I tried to imperceptibly widen them further and then wondered whether "big" was good. Completing years 4 and 5 in one year, I skipped a year at school after many visits to behavioral therapists in an attempt to understand my appalling behavior at home, such as emotional manipulation and domination, constant deception, and varying between silence and raging arguments. All I remember of the first day with the "big girls" of year 6 were my burning cheeks and the sweat on the back of my neck.

I did ballet for eleven years. In the later years, and at 5 feet and 9 inches (175 centimeters), I was taller than the other girls. Taller and less...spindly. And taller, you see, equals "bigger." I was always placed in the back row for performances. I was always designated the bigger costumes. I had no confidence, so danced clumsily and forgot routines. As girls my age dropped off in favor of netball or for social preservation, I continued for the sake of my pride. Soon I was the oldest dancing in a class of girls up to six years younger. Little prepubescent bodies in navy leotards versus my own developing one. The little girls did well. In ballet, "little" is best. Lightness of foot, lightness of body for lifting and jumping and spinning—at complete odds with my perceived physicality. I eventually stopped (a little thankfully) when my doctor told me it wasn't a good idea to do any more exercise, in an attempt to preserve the bones I was starving hollow. I folded my off-pink soft shoes into my battered *pointes* and filed them away in my wardrobe. Sometimes I take them out, trace *arabesques* and *développés*. Mostly they sleep undisturbed.

Senior school was when the private-school mold hardened and dyed itself blonde. I did not fit in any better than I did in junior school. I amused people but did not really bond with them. I taught myself to be funny, because being funny kept you somewhat socially afloat. I was the one with the goofy face and the branch of tree I named "Mabel" and hid behind the school-ground dustbin. I was the one who made up silly stories and could jerk comically. I was also the one doing well in all my subjects, and I was also the one who couldn't rebel if my life depended on it.

I spent years trying to be rebellious at school like the girls I idolized. It never worked. If I got in trouble, I didn't sulk; I flushed scarlet and apologized profusely. I stuck to the rules, taking my frustration out on my family. I didn't skip one class until I was in year 12 and very sick.

I never dyed my hair. I never used fake tan. I have, to this day, never set foot in a gym. Quite an achievement if you consider the girls I went to school with. I was absolutely hopeless with boys. My red cheeks when talking to guys were a widely held joke. I was too shy to dance, too shy to sing. And yet, I was comically a show off.

Comically, I desperately prostrated myself for attention. Comically, I masked and hopped and tried to ignore the cracks.

In year 9, my English class studied *Stick Figure* by Lori Gottlieb. It is true that the current limited awareness of eating disorders is inexcusable, that the stereotypes of sufferers (as inherently selfish, narcissistic, and purely physical) are still kicking, that most of the population has the wrong idea. It is true that the issue must be publicized and discussed. It is true, it is essential, that these stereotypes be broken. But at the time, and at that fragile age of fourteen, studying this book merely served to exacerbate a fascination with vanishing; with the whittling down of being; a gradual fading of self. In hindsight now, when I reread *Stick Figure*, the representation of an eating disorder is very … simplistic. I laugh a little, I must confess. But back then, to a self-esteem already probing its own worth, it was very potent and very swaying.

The cult of the private school strangled me. I tortured myself with my inability to be just like "them": the giggling, shrieking, nonthinking them. The "them" who attracted guys, could wear a bikini, could recite the American cheerleading movie *Bring It On* from beginning to end. The music was R 'n' B and short-skirted. The boys were private-schooled rugby players. The "books" were the magazines *Cleo* and *Cosmopolitan*. The eyebrows were professionally plucked, the legs were waxed, the mobiles were very shiny.

Boys never looked twice at me. I didn't have the right jeans. I was cringingly frigid and reserved. I didn't have the right hair or the pretty bras or *that* way of carrying myself that seemed to equal popularity. Instead, I did too well at school. I hated going out (it exposed my social ineptness). My skin was either very white or very red. I didn't run around the block in mini-shorts every afternoon, and I didn't like the beach. I thought too much and didn't speak flippantly enough. I answered enough in class for my geography teacher to draw me aside one lesson and ask me to "give the other girls a go." I had none of the sexually confident charisma everyone else seemed to have.

I was very lonely. And I came to understand that there was something intrinsically wrong with me. These were the only girls, the only surroundings, the only boys, I had ever known. Therefore *I* was the odd one out. *I* was the one who was "wrong."

Being fitted for a costume for a role in the school play, a friend turned to me and asked me what size I was.

"You're a 10, right?"

"Oh yes," I nodded.

That day, walking home from school, I realized I didn't actually know what clothing size I was. It had never occurred to me to check before. I just wore what fit me. I shut the door to my bedroom and took a dress out of the wardrobe.

It was not a size 10, and I wondered what that meant.

In year 11, I went on a school trip to Italy. There was wonderful, wonderful food. Broad beans with pecorino and olive oil, pastas, pomegranate mousse, coconut gelato; five-course meals twice a day were not uncommon. I ate everything out of politeness, as I had been taught. Our guide remarked that she liked to see my "healthy appetite." Across the table, girls pushed their pasta around and asked for a salad. I raved about this to a friend. What was their problem? We were in Italy, for God's sake, enjoy the food! But after two weeks of watching bronzed girls eat apples and sugar-free lollies bought from a highway-side supermarket, instead, I began to feel uneasy.

The academic pressure I put on myself to perform at school was extreme. It wasn't good unless my results were 100 percent, and even that wasn't good enough. I remember looking at the nicely rounded figure of 10/10 at the top of an English essay and wondering why I couldn't be more than that, why I couldn't just surpass the whole construction of "marks" altogether.

Midway through year 11, the pace changed from a hurried frustration to a speeding panic. My dear, dear grandmother died, and I was standing next to her at the moment her heart ceased to beat. I was chosen to be head prefect of my school. I was approaching the final year of my schooling, and a year in which I had to do well, because otherwise, *otherwise*, I would *never* be able to do what I wanted to do. I was going to save the world. I was going to work for the UN. I was going to be the High Commissioner for Human Rights, nay, the Secretary General. I was going to act and write and spread the awful truth of animal cruelty and factory farming. I was going to be a diplomat and one of the judges on the International Court of Justice. I was going to study at Oxford, teach in Africa, and volunteer in Romania. I was going to be an aid worker in my spare time. I would "succeed."

But success can carry with it crushing criteria, if you let it. If you expect too much from yourself, you will eventually have to confront the fact that you can only ever do as much as you *can*.

And so "something" started. I had to be very healthy for year 12, very healthy indeed. I had to eat organically. I soon decided to stop eating meat because of the appalling brutality involved. All fast food followed. I wanted to be healthier, cleaner, neater, so I could *do* more, *read* more, *achieve* more. Good God, school was stressful, and there was no way I was good enough. The girls thought I was an absolute loser. Work was everywhere. Work and notes. Unorganized, indistinct. I felt I couldn't do this. There was too much. My stomach felt strange when I thought of the exams, the HSC (Higher School Certificate). There was always a hovering panic. Oh God. Now, cut that food up. Carefully, perfectly. Play the act and keep the audience laughing. Retreat into the pillows of your bed and the pages of your diary and cry at your own falsity, at your own pretense. Why can't you just be "real"? (But there is no time, no time at all. No time for an unpeeling of self. You have work, work, work, you have work and marks and school and exams, and you must *succeed*.)

At the year 11 formal at the end of the year, a friend commented on my thin legs. I danced with and kissed a boy whose name I never asked for. I contemplated being a few kilos lighter, still. What about –kilograms? That was a nice, round, clean weight. Nice and even. Nice and contained, ordered, simple.

But of course, it is not common knowledge that if you alter your weight you alter your mind.

I'm going to lose ten kilograms, you say. *I'm going to lose ten kilograms and then I'll be exactly the same except thinner and more attractive.*

Wrong.

Everyone has a set point, a set weight, below which one ceases to think independently. I know exactly what it is for me. If I go below it, I succumb to compulsion—stuff any intention otherwise. With anorexia, we are not dealing with a superficial vanity. We are dealing with a combination of knots and anxiety unfathomable to those outside. We are dealing with a psychological mess of which weight loss is merely a symptom.

And so it started. And I refused to open my eyes.

THE DARK

A mishmash of memories

and time. . .is defunct

MEMORY 1

I always wore my jersey. I always wore my jeans. I always wore those little shoes. And I always rolled my sleeves up, so I could look at my wrists when the songs were changing on my iPod. I used to walk when the sun was setting. That way I could walk with my back to the sun and admire the way the shadows elongated and thinned my body. That gaping gap between thighs tapering down to a wasted calf. That very round head balancing on a too-thin neck. Those wrists melting into the pavement.

I listened to music, yes, but I walked to the hymn of obsession. If I try, I can still hear the swinging beat of it: one, two, three, four. My heart beating through my toes:

I. Must. Lose. Weight. I. Must. Lose. Weight. I. Must. Lose. Weight.

MEMORY 2

The swimming carnival. I wore a child's T-shirt and a red tulle skirt, and wings that kept slipping down my shoulders. All I remember now were my feet hurting on the tiles and the school principal taking a step back when she saw me. Then the deputy principal also looking at me like *that*. And my friends, who were all practicing the dance I was too weak and too tired to do, looking at me...with that very same expression. I ignored them as I ignored everything. Looked at my reflection in the glinting glass windows. Scrutinized my legs. My arms. My waist. Adjusted my wings.

MEMORY 3

A little note left on my desk. Folded coyly.

> *Dearest Lucy,*
>
> *You would make your old mum very happy if you would go to see a dietician to discuss your research on food with her and understand some of her theories and knowledge about food.*
>
> *You need a referral for a dietician, and Dr. R is available to see you at 11 a.m. on Saturday. It would be nice if you would agree to go, or otherwise I will have to insist.*
>
> *Please don't yell at me. I think we just need to find out more about what you are doing and make sure it is all right.*
>
> *All my love,*
>
> *Mummy xxxxxxxxxxxxxxxxxx*

MEMORY 4

Two appointments with two "nutritionists" then.

Appointment 1

A little office reached via steep purple stairs. A potted plant (fake) and a pile of magazines ("Love Your Body in Six Weeks!" and "Lose That Winter Flab!"). I am ushered into a little anteroom, bright, and sit on a cushioned window seat opposite a very square, very institutional scale with bright red numbers. Sally, Sue, or Susan (or I could be completely off) bounces into the room followed by her hair (very black). We talk (or she does). I say something about pasta. I start thinking about pasta. Pasta pasta pasta. Cereal. Cereal, too. She wants to weigh me. I hate this part. Pasta. Ah, pastry. Pastry pastry. Outside there is a little girl. She is staring at the wall just behind the receptionist's head. Her arms are crossed tightly against a loose gray jumper. Her hair is in a (little) bun. She's wearing pale blue jeans, but I think she forgot to put her legs on this morning. I stare and feel fat.

Appointment 2

A little office reached via stepping stones and Zen-chic pebbles. A spiky potted plant (real) and a pile of *Vogue* magazines ("Are You Pretty Enough?" and "The Season's Best New Swimsuits"). I am pointed into a larger and very white room. Another Sally, Sue, or Susan (or perhaps something else entirely) comes in and sits down. Motions I do the same, with a big, toothy smile.

I trip over my words as I tell her that I think I might be developing an eating disorder. I whisper the words, my eyes fixed on the very clean, vanilla-colored carpet. She smiles pinkly and nods her head. There is a pause.

"Well, you certainly don't look anorexic," she says.

Well, you certainly don't look anorexic. Well, *you* certainly don't look anorexic. Well, you *certainly* don't look anorexic. Well, I certainly don't *look* anorexic.

Something towards the very center of my chest spreads hotly.

Well, I'll show you, sweetheart.

MEMORY 5

Late 2004. I couldn't bring myself to walk home. I could hardly move my legs. C was the last one left in the locker room, and as she went, I felt her arms around my waist and her voice in my ear.

"Sweetheart, you're too thin."

A quick squeeze, and she was gone. I sat by my locker and cried. Looked at my blue nails with that funny bumpy bit. Pulled my hair out. Watched the squally clouds bristle and tear over North Head.

MEMORY 6

The start of 2005. Recess. Indiscriminate time. I would eat my apple. Slowly. Crunch. Crunch. Swallow. Say nothing. Watch the carpet. Field the comments. The comments...always the comments. Jokes were clumsily employed to mask a complete lack of understanding. It finally got to the stage where my classmates didn't comment anymore. The faces just looked and whispered. I found it much easier to sit by my locker and pretend to work. Stare at my shoes. Dust dry skin from the inside of my socks and skirt. Count the bones inside my uniform. I have a photo from that time. I have no body. My face is ghastly pale, with skin taut over cheekbones and skull, eyes dark and veiled, head somehow supported by a sinewy and bony mess of a neck. It's surprising now. I can hardly believe it. I couldn't see it then, and I can't fathom it now.

But that's the ugly nature of this beast. It's all a wicked lie.

MEMORY 7

I couldn't participate in the class debate. I hadn't the energy. I hadn't the brain. I sat in class silently. I watched my wrists. Just in case they got bigger. Desperately tried to quell the grumbling of my stomach. Everyone knew about my outspoken stomach. How could they not?

One memorable occasion during an English test, the comment was made:

"Was that a bus?"

The other girls laughed.

No. It was my stomach. I laughed hollowly and punched myself, hard, in the gut beneath the desk.

MEMORY 8

Drama. The floor. Some existentialist exercise involving much rolling and twitching. We were fetuses, or at least desperately attempting to be. I lay on my back and held on to my hipbones. Ran my finger up and over their hard points and half-heartedly hoped the rest of the class would notice. I turned over and winced a little as my knees hit each other.

And then all of a sudden, I didn't need to show people. Because it was painfully obvious all the time. I started trying to cover myself up.

I shrank from hugs. Especially from my family. Hugging them, I would feel them feeling my spine. My ribs. My shoulder bones. So I stopped. Stopped the hugging. Crawled inwards. Curled up, went under, didn't come out.

MEMORY 9

Mid-2005. L put her first finger and thumb around my upper arm.

"How do you keep your arms so tiny?"

I smile. I spin. I shrink away. *"They're not that tiny,"* I say, defensively. *You can't see me,* I think.

• • •

In my diary I write:

> Everything changes so suddenly—or maybe it's been gradual and I just haven't noticed. I am really lonely.

I'm not sure if I'm still losing weight or not as I can't trust the scales at home. So I'll have to wait until I see Dr. R again next week. Last Monday I managed to stay at -kilograms. She seemed relieved I had "held" from the week before, but I felt a twinge of disappointment.

I'm getting increasingly sick of everyone at school and I feel like constantly snapping, but instead just try to avoid everyone altogether. I'm really tired of remarks about my lunch. I feel so ashamed of myself for finding everyone irritating, but I'm just too tired to make the effort to rectify it.

I have been cooking a lot more, just because I find it intensely uncomfortable eating something I haven't prepared—just in case Mum or Dad try to put something really fattening or starchy in, hoping I won't notice. They think I won't notice? Sometimes I can smell fat. And besides, it's nice to follow a recipe and make food perfect. It's almost like I'm eating it myself!

I went to the funeral of a girl in my year. She was killed in a freak accident. They told us it had been sudden and painless. I sort of wish it had been my funeral. There was a girl standing near me who would not stop sniveling and spluttering and looking aggrieved. Every time someone so much as looked her way, she'd start up again. By the end I was so annoyed I felt like either asking her to sponsor Kleenex or giving her a good kick.

Instead, I watched myself from above, like I have been doing a lot of the time lately.

The library has just been inundated with a horde of twittering pink-clad year 6s, so I think I'll feign difficult work to intimidate them into silence.

Of course "work" meant staring unseeingly at bobbing words and watching time skip and drag. I never fully appreciated the minute brain processes we use every day until I lost them. For a year, over a year, my brain felt like an unreceptive blob. I could feel the weight of it, the stodginess, the sheer opacity. It was awful. For one so proud of and so dependent on her mental faculties, it was devastating. I just sat and prodded that mass feebly. Melted into torpor for half an hour, an hour. Poke. Melt. Poke. Melt.

MEMORY 10

A very private conversation with Mr. S. I watch his glasses as he tells me that he expects me to be the best drama student he's ever had. He tells me he won't be happy with any Drama mark under –. *"Higher,"* he says.

I sit, I blush, I sweat.
No. I'm sorry.
I'll try to die instead.

• • •

In my diary I write:

I've lost –kilos. My thighs are still fat though.

MEMORY 11

In drama class I was a barefooted Mary Tyrone in Eugene O'Neill's hauntingly powerful play *Long Day's Journey into Night.* Mary is horribly addicted to drugs, and the play's terrifying portrayal of her descent and psychological absence struck a chord with me. Hair out, eyes smudged, a mirror in one hand. The lines ebbed. My lips stopped. Hand to waist, feel the space. Flat. Contained. It's okay. Still thin. See? I'm not fixed. I continued…just as fucked and volatile as before.

MEMORY 12

In a doctor's office, I compared my arms with those of the chair as she said, "There's nothing more I can do for you, Lucy. You're beyond my help. I've made an appointment for you with a specialist. She's the best in Sydney. Specializes in eating disorders."

Her voice hummed and faded with pity. Pity and sympathy. My skin crawled. I cried half-heartedly, weakly.

Later, the black dog. I writhe on my bed. I scream. I cry. I can't remember what was said. I called for Mum. She came. In my memory the room appears in a sort of distilled oval. The black spilling in from my mind out. Those who have seen, have felt, have been…will know that that does make sense. Simultaneously from within and without. Suffocating.

• • •

In my diary I write:

> As I believe I don't actually have a problem, I feel I need to justify all the specialist appointments and money being spent on me by losing enough weight until I do actually have a problem…

A day later I was in the specialist's office. Cold sunlight, potted plants. Did my calves look bigger if I squished them against the underside of the sofa?

"Oh, Lucy. Things are looking grim. You're going to have to go to hospital."

I was momentarily distracted from my fevered observation of the size of my calves. I sat there, blankly. My hands found comfort in the bones of each elbow. Huddled. Hospital? I blubbered incoherently. No. No, no, no, this is all a big mistake. Shouldn't this doctor be spending time with girls who were actually anorexic? No. Not hospital. No. I couldn't do that. Give me one more chance, just one more chance. A week. The specialist looked at me sharply. Hard. For a long time. And let me go, putting me at the top of the waiting list anyway. Waiting for a bed. A bed, a bed. A bed and blood tests. Force-feeding. Isolation and whispered competition. Crying, futility.

I told no one, but hugged the threat of hospital to my chest like a soft bomb.

MEMORY 13

Upstairs, in my bedroom, I wrapped my hands around my upper thigh.

"Look, Mum! Look at that!"

She looks. I stare in wonder. She starts to cry. I drop my hands guiltily and creep downstairs.

· · ·

In my diary I write:

> I've dropped again. I don't feel anything. Apparently my weight is so low for my height that I'm eating myself (brain included). But it just doesn't make sense. It's a sterile, passionless statement. It's all so fucking perverse. And bewildering! I feel so detached. I've spent so long analyzing it I don't know what to think anymore. I just can't see what they're seeing. Occasionally I'll catch a fleeting glimpse of myself in a car window or shop door and step back in horror. But then, flesh will grow back and hide the skeleton, and no amount of squinting will bring it back.
>
> I'm scared of what I'm doing to myself, but I'm not sure how to stop. I'm in such excellent control of myself around food that I really don't want to have to be in the situation of having to put on weight. But I seem to have lost the ability to maintain my weight—the only thing I know how to do is lose it and make me smaller. I feel like I've been plunged into hell without a breather.
>
> I dreamt last night that I was dying and Mum and Dad decided to hurry it along and guillotine me in the lounge room. Mum was going to cremate me and I remember wanting my Snoopy burnt with

me and forget-me-nots on my casket and thinking that I'd be able to spend next Christmas next to my grandmother's ashes under the brown cabinet in the dining room.

I think I'm terrified. Secretly, I'm crumbling. I don't know how to get out.

MEMORY 14

At night my mind paraded a feast of immense proportions behind my eyelids, and I'd lie awake for hours. I would drift into sleep, dreaming of food. Dreaming of eating. Waking in a panic, I'd feel my hipbones, count my ribs—and relax slightly as I realized it was just a dream.

MEMORY 15

Going to bed hurt. Sleeping hurt. Too many angles digging into the mattress. I developed a system of bizarre positions to shield my shoulders, hips, and ribs from bruising themselves. Then I'd stay in the same position all night. Lying there, always cold, left hand measuring the space between my legs when I lay on my side. More than yesterday? Last week? A month ago? I was obsessed. Obsessed with creating spaces and holes and gaps. Turning something into nothing. Melting what had been there into the air and into the past.

● ● ●

In my diary I write:

Another antidepressant. How many has it been? This one's technically an antipsychotic. I'm...pretty low right now. I can feel it physically descending. I am faint. My mouth tingles. It's strange. More hair is falling out and I'm always, always cold. My bones are cold. The coldness scrabbles icily from the inside, out.

But I'm still fat.

My brain feels more and more logical and true as others tell me it is more and more irrational. Everything is bizarre. Sometimes I feel as though something is trying to live through me; through my brain. I'm scaring myself. Yesterday I cut myself again with my little razor and Mum walked in. I was cornered and felt so hopelessly, hopelessly weak.

I've felt awful all day today—just so isolated.

No one ever notices anything. People think it's terrible to think of all the people dying all the time, but I think it's more depressing to think of all the people being born all the time. I cried in the school bathroom for a little while, which made me feel better, but now if someone looks at me again, I think I'll just burst into tears.

I have managed to phase out eating so completely that I don't even have cravings anymore. The panic and disgust I feel when I have a mouth full of food is unbelievable, and I'm gripped by an absolute need to get rid of it—hiding it anywhere and everywhere if only I don't have to swallow. It's only when every last smear of taste is gone from my mouth, from under my tongue, my throat, that my heart stops racing. I feel so ashamed, but I need the other girls to see that I have a problem. I don't know why. Perhaps it is to impress on them that I am more than what they see at school—that I have concerns and complexities and pain. Perhaps there is a performance element—almost like I have become this great sideshow and don't want to disappoint.

Watch me leap and plunge. Watch me fade into nothing.

MEMORY 16

Trying to read *Portrait of a Lady*? Don't do it when you're anorexic, depressed, and prone to moments of utter vacuity. My eyes lingered over every single word painfully. One sentence gone. Okay. That went in, I think. A paragraph. My brain would swim and refuse to concentrate. A word. Hah. Look at that word. Ten minutes later, hang on, it's the same word. That's really weird.

A month later, the same chapter. Sometimes the same page.

I spent so much time looking at the woman in the painting on the cover. Thinking about her. My one complaint against Henry James is that he doesn't talk about food enough. I needed long digressions detailing banquets and feasts with stuffed pigeon (despite the vegetarianism), piles of roasted vegetables, softly cooked eggs, cheeses, fruits, and bubbling cherry pies. It took me twelve months of reading every night to finish that goddamned book. I haven't picked it up since I put it away. I can't.

I saw that cover in a bookshop three days ago. Stood there and stared. Transfixed again by the lady on the cover. I stood there until a blonde woman elbowed her way past me to the paperback romances section. My eyes slipped to Camus instead, not without a sigh.

• • •

In my diary I write:

> Note to self: DO NOT drink four black Smirnoffs (equal to nine drinks) back-to-back on an empty stomach whilst on antidepressants and severely underweight. Very ugly.

My friends weren't quite sure what to do with me. I spent the rest of my year 12 formal after-party with my head in my hands, fighting swells of panic and vertigo.

MEMORY 17

I stayed up most of last night. I couldn't stop fainting into the sink.

I swayed into the bathroom and sat on the toilet, my hands gripping the basin weakly, my head lolling. Waves. Waves of consciousness. Yellow light. A heave of goose bumps. Stumbled back into bed and clutched the covers. Woke in the morning in a cold huddle of sweat. Peeled the pajamas off. Watched the stars rise and fall.

MEMORY 18

Suicide watch. I do tend to forget about this. The weeks my parents were ordered never to leave me alone have melted into a muted expanse of half-life. My dietician later told me that she would watch me every time I left an appointment and honestly wonder if she would see me alive again.

Part of me did, too.

In my diary I write:

> I want to die. I want to die. I want to disappear and never worry again and not be a burden on anyone else anymore. I want to kill myself. I want desperately to get thinner and thinner and fade into nothingness. Very low and black. I wonder what it is like to die. I feel nothing but a black-settled blankness. The anorexia speaks. I'm weak and I listen. It hates me for giving in to everything. If only I could vanish. I want to strangle, scratch, pull, and squeeze the life out of me. Why keep any of me? It's so useless.

MEMORY 19

While I waited for an appointment with my psychiatrist in the inpatient ward at an eating disorder center, I watched the skeletal girls who looked like they might snap, with eyes veiled and strangely motionless, like a dark, still pond. They looked at me, with those hungry, dissatisfied eyes, and I started crying because I knew they were all thinking that I was fat and wondering what I was doing there.

There was a woman who lived near me who was literally bone with thin, wrinkled skin stretched over the crevices. She always wore black tights and this oversized, yellow zip-up jumper. She always walked with her head bowed, but there was a sort of defiance in her step. My heart ached every time I saw her. She once carried home a jar of Nutella from the supermarket. I stood on the corner, my heart uncomfortable in my throat, and watched her until she strode around the bend.

I haven't seen her since.

MEMORY 20

A poem. I don't think it has any literary merit whatsoever. I wrote as I felt and that was that. Now, when I read over what I scribbled down in hungry slumps, I cringe. I cry too, to be honest. The words scare me.

Ana's Poem
It is what I expected:
Shadowed and black.
A void.
Jagged ridges jut precariously
From the pitted jet walls.
Bones.
There are bones.
Pearly and smooth
They protrude

Through flesh.
They are clean
Perfect
Stripped of ugliness.
Whittled down,
The bones stand
Pure and flawless:
The essence of being.
It is lonely here.
Others speak in muffled voices
I try to cry but gag.
There is nothing I can do.
I have yielded;
My soul is confined
Within a barren cage
Of denial.
It is dark.
The ridges rear;
The silence deafens.
The yawning blackness
Stretches downward further
And further.
It doesn't stop.
It goes around,
Swirling,
In blackened spirals:
A gothic lollypop.
It is empty here.
Devoid of feeling.
It is what I expected
But it is not as it used to be.
Pillaged
And numbed
Life flutters
Somewhere in the gloom
But it cannot be heard. The blackness growls;
Life quivers;
And goes out.

• • •

In my diary I write:

> If the depression continues like this for much longer, I'll be locked up in hospital anyway.
>
> I'm walking out in front of cars. They keep fucking missing me.
>
> This is so painful. Wrenching something from yourself that you believe to be an integral part of your identity is painful. Very. What would I be without anorexia? Will there be anything left? I have gagged myself for so long I can't remember a pre-anorexic time. Anorexia is my reality. Losing weight is my reality. It is the only thing I can do. I have sacrificed my brain, I have sacrificed my friends, and I have sacrificed any remnant of self. So what can I do?

Lose weight, of course. Easy-peasy. That was something I could do, and do well.

MEMORY 21

The colorful cavalcade of antidepressants. That glass box of existence with the screaming depression on all sides. A flimsy smear of artificial happiness, the pretending of an emotion so transparent and so untrue. I would laugh and laugh and laugh, hysterically. Then cry. Tears and shuddering sobs. Standing on the edge of a sheer precipice, I could wobble either way. Hours. Hours of acrobatic emotions, leaping from terrifying elation to heartbreaking despair. In the space of a second. Then I would sleep.

MEMORY 22

I stood and glared at my father in the hallway. Red-faced, grappling with the terrifyingly foreign: a daughter smiling at death. Neither of us would concede defeat. We're each as stubborn and hot-tempered as the other, and by God we've had some roaring showdowns. I have no memory of the context of this argument (which was just one among many), but I do remember the finale.

"If you continue to carry on this way, do you know what you are?" he sputtered. *"You're fucked in the head. That's what you are."*

I turned on my heel and left. Slammed the gate to my mother's worried protestations and my father's huffed fear. I walked. And walked, and walked. Walked away the pain; walked away the terror. They'll learn. I clenched my white hands in tiny fists until they ached, until the bones felt they might bow. They'll learn soon enough that this isn't a fucking game. I pounded up hill after hill, in some attempt to purge myself of the emotion; that alien heat I had learnt to numb.

Oh God, what have I done?

MEMORY 23

–kilograms. I felt claustrophobic, hemmed in, netted. I felt gray and black; I felt cold; emptiness; hunger; edges. I had annexed my soul and watched this compelling stumble toward self-destruction with a half smile. I was not me, and that body was certainly not mine. Self-annihilation is ridiculously compelling. How far can she go? I was my own morbid entertainment. A disembodied denial warped everything. I asked my psychiatrist to please stop seeing me, so she could spend time with real anorectics and people who were actually seriously ill.

"Absolutely not," she said. *"Because that's what you are."*

• • •

In my diary I write:

> I'll probably have to go to hospital. I don't really see why that is necessary. I wish people would just calm down and be rational. I'm not that thin.
>
> This is ridiculous. I'm technically classified anorexic but I find this very difficult to believe. I mean, how can two people see two such different versions of something

directly in front of them? It doesn't make any rational sense. Eyes are eyes and a mirror is a mirror...

. . .

If you want to be anorexic, this is what you have to be prepared for: the stomach pain, the heart flutters, the blackness, the uncomfortable nights because every way you turn your bones stick into the bed, the constant accusing and pathetically pitiful stares, the crying, the friends who abandon you, your school marks which plummet, a brain that does nothing but think food, food, food, being kept awake every night planning what you'll eat the next day and then not going to sleep because you are so hungry, the nightmares about gorging yourself on food from which you wake up crying, the handfuls of hair that come out and cover everything, the blue and lumpy fingernails, the unhealable bruises, the goose bumps, the cold, the absolute obsession with cooking and feeding other people, the self-hate, the loneliness, clothes that will never fit no matter what size, the constipation, the awful depression when you've finished your tiny breakfast and realize there are four hours to go until lunch, or when you finish lunch and realize you have to wait six hours for dinner, then fourteen hours overnight...

You will stop talking, listening to music, seeing your friends, patting your dog, planning your life, dreaming, doing work, feeling happy, going on the Internet, reading, watching TV (except for the cooking channel) ... you will stop living. You will find no pleasure in anything. You will be moody. You will never laugh and you will rarely smile, except with pride, perhaps, as the scales drop lower.

Then will come the continuous doctors' appointments and the ultimatum: put on weight or drop out of school and be an invalid for the rest of your life before you eventually die of starvation and/or heart failure. It will be torturous. The antidepressants will feel like they are killing you. You will lie in bed for days unable to move. You will not care about anything but holding on to the anorexia. You would prefer to die. You will try to die.

Then the refeeding (horrible, horrible word) will begin. You will panic whenever you have food in your mouth. The anorexia will shriek at you to get it out, to spit it down the drain, scrape it from your teeth and walk around the block for good measure. You will hate yourself with such a passion that you will want to rip the fat off, shred it and tear it, cause yourself as much pain as possible. Then you will realize that you cannot kill yourself now because you wouldn't be thin enough in the coffin. People would walk past and murmur, "Oh! Wasn't she fat!" It will fail to register that you are still severely anorexic at this point and will be for some time.

Sometimes you will see yourself in the mirror and briefly gasp with horror at the sight of your own bones. And then truth will melt into delusion, and your thighs will spring back and your stomach will bulge over rippled ribs and you will feel horribly normal once more. You will be scared to go outside just in case your utter grossness is spotted by someone else. God forbid they should see those arms or that face. You will feel like a nobody, a worthless nonperson who deserves nothing, has nothing, is nothing. The depression may swallow you in its blackness. You will withdraw from everything. You will spend hour after hour lying motionless on your bed, suffocating under a black cloud, hating yourself with a sheer intensity incomprehensible to those on the outside, willing yourself to get up and burn off that sordid food you were forced to eat. But you will be too tired. You will not be able to physically raise your head.

This will continue, for some time. Months will melt away into nothing. But somewhere...through the black and the gray and the cold... there is a light.

I can see it, now.

THE GRAY

In which Lucy straggles along, albeit not quite keeping her head up

I have always kept a diary. My initial reason of preserving the minutiae of my tea-partied and lacy childhood has long since faded, and now I use it to purge my thoughts, rather than my food. I chuck the day's psychological residue into a virtually incoherent tangle on my computer from my journal, and sift through it, knitting ideas and patterns, desperately trying to understand the "why" of everything.

But first, I feel an extenuating treatise is in order. I need to explain something. I need to explain "school" to you, as it pertained to me.

School.

I am in no way "cool" and at school it was no different. I was awkward and I was odd. I was entertaining, so I was saved the social massacre of being labeled a true geek. I threw myself entirely into my work because it was the only way I could prove any smattering of self-worth.

Perhaps I became a little too obsessed with marks. Perhaps I was a little too concerned with how the teachers saw me and how my peers reacted to me. "I" was found in little piles of scribbled paper with perfect marks clapping at the top; "I" could be seen making a fool of myself for that holy grail of popular laughter. But "I" as distinct, as separate, as autonomous? Nope. Didn't exist. I was as I was seen. That is all.

I was fiercely competitive. I enjoyed exams. I had to be at the top of the class, or else I was effectively rendered worthless. I was worth only as much as my mark, and if it was below par, then "I" was below par, and "I" was in no position to speak to anyone, let alone the "plastics." (My peers, as I perceived them to be. Blonde and glossed, perfectly put together and tanned to within an inch of their lives; I used this label with a mixture of searing jealousy and disgust.)

Anorexia demanded certain changes. Firstly, I had to understand that I, quite frankly, had more important things to worry about than a successful future, the foremost being the dissolution of self. Secondly, I had to appreciate that I did not need anyone else in this pursuit of perfection. Thirdly…thirdly, I had to sacrifice my brain to a starving body: that is, literally and biologically eat it. The result being that I hadn't the energy to speak in class, to read my books, to concentrate on study. My handwriting shook across the page, sometimes illegibly, always too small to read. I could not "stream" essays—they came instead in lumps and stops. Words eluded me. Simple concepts would not stick to my brain. Midway through conversations, I would forget why I was there, whom I was talking to, or what we were talking of. Walking up stairs, in particular, I would swing in and out of my body, half aware and half dead to the sensation.

My marks began to falter. I looked blindly at the far-from-perfect marks on my very short essays and fumbled excuses. I would go home and cry weakly. I abandoned my ambition for sugar-free gum and extra walking. I was a failure. I couldn't "do" "it"—whatever that was. So…if I was going to start falling, I might as well do it properly. I might as well be a display of überanorexia. Above par at starving. A perfect mark in self-destruction. Uh-oh. A new idea of self forged. And it's DIY! Not so healthy, this one.

As entirely as I sacrificed my marks, my ambition, my expectations of a brilliant future, it seemed as though nothing could blunt my academic pride. It was this that caused me the most pain. Memories of how I used to be, how people expected me to be brilliant—how I expected myself to be brilliant—cut away. The fact that I was head prefect and supposed to give an extraordinary address to thousands on Speech Night later that year, that I was expected to be at the top of my class, that I was supposed to do fantastically and get straight into Arts/Law at Sydney University…and the fact that I simply felt I couldn't, jarred horrifically. I have never felt so much personal pain. I was failing—and not for unpreventable circumstances, but because I was starving myself.

I don't know what else to say. Staying at school and watching myself fall to others was one of the hardest things I have ever done.

Pride is ruthless.

It also saved me.

When I couldn't fathom dropping out of school; when I cried myself into breathlessness at the thought of having to repeat my final year, of not sitting my final exams, of Failing to Succeed and Get Where I Wanted to Go; when I realized that I was actually not only killing myself (that was a secondary concern), but that I would embarrass my expectations and have to concede defeat, I took my first furtive, and painful step back from the edge.

It is indescribably difficult, writing this. I cannot seem to find words for how excruciating choosing between anorexia and life was. This will not make sense to you, or perhaps it (unfortunately) will. But I have never, ever battled psychologically something so merciless.

Anorexia is not some fad self-gratuitous diet. It isn't an exercise in vanity or a shortcut to *Cosmopolitan*'s perfect summer bikini body. It is an obsession, a compulsion. It is self-injury—but we cut our brains and our souls, not our wrists.

Again, there are no dates for the following part. I was severely underweight. I could not see this; I could not feel this. All I knew was that I had put on a few kilos from my low weight. Time was measured in the hours between meals; the hours gone without food; the hours spent walking. The passing of the seasons was irrelevant. I was always cold. Monday was Wednesday was Sunday was April was August. You will notice, of course, the differences between the earlier journal entries and the later ones. The differences in perception, in style, in thought. That my brain withdrew is patent. That it eventually peeked out and saw colors is too.

. . .

I'm going to "trial" recovery. The idea of indeterminate life is terrifying. I will get through my HSC and maybe my degree. Then I will go back to anorexia if I am the same and unchanged. That is a comfort. I have a way out.

I wonder what the next few weeks will be like; what putting on weight will be like. I wonder what I'm like, underneath it all. Or even if I have a likeness. Maybe nothing's there.

. . .

I can make my thighs press together sometimes when I'm standing. I do it out of fascination that I could have allowed myself to get so big. I feel like crying with desperation. Tonight I stood in the supermarket, next to a heap of dusty sleeping potatoes, squeezing my thighs. Squeeze. Touch. Squeeze. Touch. Crawling goose bumps of panic. Discreetly slip the low-fat vanilla custard back into its place next to the soymilk and double cream.

You don't need that.

. . .

My shopping list for when I eventually leave home:
- *no-fat yogurt in various flavors*
- *1 carton low-fat vanilla custard*
- *mustard—Dijon and seeded*
- *low-fat Philadelphia cream cheese*
- *heavy seed bread in small slices (Burgen)*
- *low-calorie flatbread*
- *coffee*
- *carrots and celery—to be cut up into sticks*
- *green apples (sour)*

- *no-fat soymilk*
- *tofu*
- *borlotti beans for protein*
- *small cans corn kernels and baby corn*
- *rice crackers—fairly tasteless ones*
- *Diet Coke*
- *flavored water*
- *low-calorie hot chocolate (to be made with water)*
- *tea bags (rooibos and vanilla; peppermint; Earl Grey)*
- *Weet-bix*
- *frozen low-fat yogurts*
- *sweet chili sauce (to put on everything)*
- *Vegemite for vitamins*
- *block of thin 85 percent dark chocolate*
- *fruit (lots; esp. pineapple, watermelon, strawberries, pears, plums, mangos)*
- *vegetables (except potatoes and parsnips and eggplant)*
- *organic low-cal cereal*
- *Special K*

Everyone thinks I'm finally starting to get better, but they cannot possibly understand how much this grates. I don't want to get better. I desperately, desperately want the anorexia. I need a drive, a comfort, a blindfold. I'm scared K won't like me anymore because I'm not anorexic. Life's a double-edged sword at the moment: my mood soars and plunges, and I feel very, very alone.

. . .

The HSC exams, and I've lost 1.5 kilograms from the semi-perhaps-I'll-think-about-recovering weight I've been maintaining at for a month or so. I can't seem to write essays anymore. They used to flow thematically and now they just stop and start—with an emphasis on the stopping. I find gathering my thoughts almost painful. Plans don't make sense. I'll lose myself toward the end of a sentence and not be able to remember how I was going to finish it. Sometimes I blank out and realize later that I've been staring fixedly at the blue plastic table for ten minutes. I find the red ticking second hand on the clock endlessly fascinating. I can barely stand to look away. My head doesn't feel like it's mine.

I used to love exams. There used to be nothing I enjoyed more than a good prickly essay within time limits. And now, at the most important ones, I trip up, and momentarily lose the precious weight I've gained as "brain food." Not clever, Lucy. Not clever at all.

•　•　•

I spent most of today talking to Mum about the possibility of failure in my life. About how most people are content to be "a hairdresser" or "an accountant" or "a lawyer." About how if I do Law at university, it's because I want to be the head of the UN. Or at least the High Commissioner for Human Rights. My mind is ruled by ambition. So I'm doomed to fail, really. My happiness is directly resultant from my perceived success, and I can never win because I'm just not good enough anyway.

•　•　•

I had to sleep in the middle of the English extension exam. I just couldn't take it. Luckily, I have provisions that allow for a twenty-minute "rest break." So I laid my head down on the cool desk, closed my eyes, and tried to block out the scratching pen to my front. I was just so exhausted. My brain was wobbling in its own stupor. I have never felt so helpless, so weak, or so disappointing before in my life.

I closed my eyes and everything was white behind my eyelids.

I opened them twenty minutes later and everything was blue.

I've written my speech for speech night. It was approved, if hesitantly. I'm going to speak about anorexia. I think it's important.

•　•　•

Brain paralysis. The psychological equivalent of an electrical blackout. Except my brain/empty-head-space adopts a sticky, fogged white. It's really peculiar. I just blank out. The exams are making it even harder. I can barely discern myself from the exam paper, or the answer booklet or the carpet. I feel so horribly flattened and a nonentity.

I feel very alone. Very…distanced. I wonder if anyone will ever love me. The only guys I've ever met are metaphorical inflated rugby balls. Big, ballsy, and full of air.

• • •

History exam tomorrow. Am suffering a kind of elongated brain-fart. Haven't covered nature and impact of Pol Pot's regime over democratic Kampuchea yet. Difficult. Can't think to save my life. Sleep instead. Have nothing intelligent to say.

• • •

What's with life, anyway? The billions of people and other animals in the world, each with their own little life, little concerns, little colors; breathing and feeling…it's amazing but so depressing. I can only ever be little floppy me. I can't save the world, and I'll die hardly having seen any of it.

That bloody fly won't stop its incessant kamikazic wheeling. Hopefully it will scald itself on the light bulb.

Question: If matter can be neither created nor destroyed, then what happens to the weight we lose?

• • •

I've binged terribly today. This is what I ate:

- *1 fruit bun (sort of the size of a hot-cross bun but slightly smaller)*
- *1 date*
- *1 stuffed olive*
- *1 bit of cheese*
- *1 little tub of boysenberry yogurt*
- *some stewed rhubarb*
- *a spoonful of muesli*
- *1 low-fat chocolate mousse*
- *3 cashews*

- *1 beetroot slice*

- *a cube of fresh pineapple*

- *a spoonful of coffee gelato.*

I feel so sick. And so, so desperately lonely. Mum looked terribly sad when I went, crying, to her about my binge.

"Lucy," she said, *"that's hardly anything."*

I just don't understand. I scream it, sometimes. I JUST DON'T UNDERSTAND ANY OF THIS.

• • •

I have finished my HSC.

I have finished *the* HSC.

And I feel absolutely nothing.

• • •

That's it. That's it. My hair is stuck to my cheeks with tears. A whole part of me has finished. A feeling of heady liberation and utter redundancy. Speech night: over. School: over. My speech as head prefect to two thousand parents and girls and teachers: over. To all those who failed to support me, who told me to just give up and drop out of school to save myself the effort, who cared more about asking me to "pull up my socks" than how I was, as I stumbled, bone-thin and gray, down school corridors…this speech was as much for them as it was for anyone else.

> *…Never, never, never give up.* [I mentioned that this concept holds a searing personal significance.]
>
> *I battled anorexia for much of this year.*
>
> *And if there is anything that I have learnt from that nightmare, it is to never give up. To struggle on despite obstacles. To implicitly believe in your own ability. To pay no heed to the people or mental barriers around that who would trip you up. To carry on. Girls, you can do whatever you put your mind to. I'm a living, breathing example of that. With a bit of determination, faith, and inner-conviction, you will make it wherever you want to go. Never doubt yourself. Reach for the highest stars possible. Yes, it's a struggle, I won't deny that. But nothing worth having comes without a struggle. History itself teaches us that! I look*

around tonight and look at you…and I see our future. Our future engineers, lawyers, sportswomen, politicians, teachers, mothers, gastroenterologists…you girls are sparkling with talent.

We also lost one of our own wonderful girls earlier this year. But, I know in my heart, that we have made her proud. Despite the overwhelming grief and anger, we fought on. In the face of such senseless tragedy, we battled on and banded together. We struggled at times, but…we made it. We never gave up.

It is also easy to grow disillusioned with the world we live in and the humanity of which we are a part. But we mustn't. This year, we have faced natural and man-made disasters in the form of a devastating tsunami, earthquakes, hurricanes, bombings, and war. Our faith and that of others may have been battered, our resilience tested, but humanity's determination and will have prevailed. Hope still glistens despite the darkness. And while there is determination, there is hope.

Never give up. Never forfeit your dreams. Don't be disillusioned by failure or disappointment—they can only ever be temporary. Struggle on and strain further for that star. And it is this message that epitomizes our school's legacy. To carry on in the face of adversity, whether personal, professional, or social, is one of the most powerful lessons we can learn and one of the most powerful messages we can give. Thomas Carlyle said that "the block of granite, which was an obstacle in the path of the weak, becomes a stepping stone in the path of the strong."

My block of granite hasn't quite become my stepping stone. But I'm almost there. And I'm not giving up. There is another quote I always turn to when I'm feeling discouraged: "Strength doesn't always roar, sometimes strength is the quiet voice at the end of the day saying, 'I will try again tomorrow and never, ever, ever give up.'"

I turned. I felt a collective hum wash over the hall. I took my books and walked down the stairs. All I can remember seeing were my black school shoes, polished, against the parquet floor and thinking whether or not carrying my books like-so would make my arms look thinner, so people didn't turn to each other with raised eyebrows and mumble, "Well, she doesn't *look* anorexic." So I could maintain some smattering of credibility. I didn't hear the applause, didn't see the girls standing, could not discern one face from the anonymous swirl. I just felt shuttered and choked back tears in the bright lights.

But now, I feel…clear. I am absolutely, entirely, head-splittingly knackered. But it's all over. I cleared the air and finally told them all.

The whole past year feels like a nightmarish sequence of episodes seemingly disconnected…yet so closely aligned. A nightmare-behind-glass.

Low. Gray. Down. I've been crying ever since I came home. I just want to be frail, fragile, breakable. Bones perfected. Sometimes I just wish I had no family or ambition or brain or pride, so I could go back to anorexia with no regrets and no return. Tonight has really affected me. I'm over this "life." I almost couldn't care.

• • •

I feel…brittle today. Pretty low. I generally feel like this the day after a night of alcohol, but there's this certain veil of surrealism as well. *I just can't believe everything is over.* I've spent twelve years of school working up to this point, and in the last year and a half, I trip over myself.

(Bedroom, bed, blankets. Night. Lucy is dressed in her underwear only. She sits up at the end of her bed, over her lamp.)

> **Rational Lucy:** Honestly, Luce, given the circumstances, what you did this past year is almost unbelievable, considering you almost died. And still could, really.

> **Emotional Lucy flecked with anorexic sentiment:** Where would I be if I had been functioning unimpeded this year? How high could I have gone?

I don't revel in the fact that I meticulously fostered my own defeat this year.

I feel selfish because I should be thrilled. I mean, I survived year 12. Instead, I'm being whined at by overactive perfectionism and an academic pride I sacrificed long ago to an eating disorder.

So this is what I did: As no one was home, I ran around the house screaming and dancing crazily for a few minutes. That made me feel better. Then I had a rice pudding. Then I talked to the TV for a while. Then I lectured myself. Then I pretended to be a famous actor giving an interview to my attentive reflection. Then I went up to the shops. Tried on two dresses. Want both dresses. Incidentally can't pay for both dresses. Decide I will blackmail Mum into buying them for me tomorrow.

Came home and ate some walnuts, chocolate mousse, and some cheese. Then a slightly under-ripe mango, just for the heck of it. Laughed at all the miserable-looking models on the fashion channel. Hated them for their legs. Turned the depressing show off and went to tackle my dog on Mum's bed. Got hungry, so aimlessly watched TV whilst eating seeded mustard from the jar with a spoon. Maintained this for half an hour. Felt sick.

Fell asleep. Woke up. Tried to forget about exam marks. Whiled away time uselessly on the Internet trying to find out some way to hack into other peoples' marks. Didn't succeed.

Pondered the meaning of life. Followed despondently after Mum when she came home. Decided to eat dinner at 4:30 p.m. Had some Attiki yogurt, organic cereal with blueberries, three sultanas, another slice of cheese, half a can of baby corn, a mushroom, and a few glasses of water.

Went out driving. Actually managed to turn a few corners without crashing the car or somebody else's. Saw some lovely boys with their shirts off and did the best curve of my life. Collected Thai takeaway. It attacked me, so I ate some. Watched the news.

• • •

I tell you, ripping up old and decrepit math textbooks really is the most cathartic thing. It's just lovely to see all those surds and irrational numbers on the floor in little bits.

• • •

I will not let the past few years defeat me. I am going to apply to study Arts/Law at Sydney University anyway. With special consideration, perhaps I have a chance. Here is my personal statement upon my application to Sydney University:

> *This year I have had the immense privilege of being Head Prefect at...School. The role involved much organizational skill*

and oratory persuasion in leading the twenty-five prefects and representing the school at various functions. My academic studies are, however, my prime focus, despite my many ambitions being thwarted by the onset of anorexia and severe depression in mid 2004. My reverence for English and History has remained with me nonetheless, despite the circumstances. Writing my Four Unit English major work and focusing on nineteenth-century literature (English Extension 1) and John Donne's poetry (Advanced English) were highlights for me, as was the core study of World War I in History. I am currently on a dual academic and language (Latin) scholarship.

I was awarded Dux in year 11 (including a mark of 100 percent in English) and in year 9, and also received the end-of-year prize for writing for my portfolio of literary work. I have debated from year 9 (regrettably having to stop this year due to my illness) and I have participated in the Mock United Nations Assembly (MUNA) and National Young Leaders Programme. I was the Editor of the school newspaper, which I loved as I was able to project issues that distressed me, such as animal cruelty, to the wider community. I have also been a Peer Support Leader and was fortunate enough to complete my work experience at the District Court of New South Wales under the guidance of Judge…QC, where I experienced the legal system firsthand and dealt with clients. I volunteered at the Cat Protection Society for several months and had the chance to go on a school history tour of Italy in April last year. Acting is another of my interests, and I have taken part in Australian Theatre for Young People workshops over the years.

My ambition is to be a Human and Animal Rights Lawyer for the United Nations, or the United Nations High Commissioner for Human Rights. Another avenue which has always fascinated me is that of an academic at Oxford University, where I intend to continue my studies post Sydney University. I believe Arts/Law at Sydney University will provide me with an unassailable basis for a future career in the Humanities and Law.

If I get in, it will be a miracle.

• • •

Life feels like an elasticated, gray dream. A roll of loneliness and inadequacy. I want to somehow translate my deep personal dissatisfaction onto something, and my body is an easy target. I can easily etch my hurt in bones and gaps and stretched skin and hollowed eyes. I want to be skeletal again. I want to be emaciated. I want to starve myself into utter oblivion. I want to wither and fade. It's easier than just telling people about the darkness.

Maybe I want people to see that I'm not impervious. I can't do everything. I do have holes. I'm not always crazy-little-Lucy with another goofy smile, amusing body spasm, face twitch or noise. I am human, and I am a damaged one at that.

I am not fucking perfect. I'm sick of the act.

Words
Words
Sludge and suck.
It's quite interesting, actually,
Trying to prod the bog of the mind
Into action.
Because, you see,
You can prod and prick and poke
But nothing happens.
It just sits there.

Words sink and fold back
Reality seems to bear little relation
To anything;
Least of all myself.

Breathing exhausts me. It's so heavy.

• • •

I wrote a letter to my parents after a raging argument in Jervis Bay (a regular weekend holiday spot, the "holiday" of which is somehow translated in my parents' minds as "a holiday from healthy food and a chance to eat a load of expensive, buttery shit"). It contained the following points:

1. *I want you to understand that I'm finding recovery very, very difficult. I don't tell you everything. I think you already know that. I am trying my absolute hardest. I've put on –kilograms since my lowest weight. I think that's impressive.*

2. *I think you misunderstand the power of anorexia. I think you think it is some vanity-worshipping, self-pitying illness that can be snapped out of at will. It isn't. It's an addiction. And like any addiction, it takes time to overcome.*

3. *To be completely truthful, I also don't think you understand anorexia as a psychological illness. The previous scholarly work that has been done on it, the works that you may have read, are outdated. Specialists are coming to understand that they're not dealing with it effectively, and that what they'd always thought it was about, is wrong. There is a lot of research being carried out at the moment into the best way to deal with and treat anorexic patients. The traditional approach is ineffective, wrong, and focuses on attitudes held by bewildered parents and doctors. Not of the sufferers themselves.*

4. *Please don't try to pretend that you know more about this than I do. Why do you think I spend so much time on the Internet? I read. And read and read. Articles, research, information, diagnoses. I talk to other girls with anorexia. I write in my own online journal about my experience. I cruise through pro-ana and pro-recovery sites trying desperately to work out why this horror exists. I want to help others.*

5. *I understand why you're responding to this the way you are. You're scared and don't know how to deal with me supposedly self-destructing in front of you. I'm not. I was, but now I'm not. Now, I'm just searching for the meaning of this whole thing, so I can understand it better.*

6. *I need you to understand that the days of me eating "normally"*
    and "care-freely" won't come around for quite a while yet.
    I simply can't do it. I need you to let me eat independently.
    From my research, I've also decided (and I'll be asking my
    psychiatrist about this) that the way people traditionally eat
    is not particularly healthy. The three solid meals a day thing
    can't work for me at this present point. I can't go from where
    I was to that this quickly. You may have read somewhere
    that recovery takes many years. The few months I have been
    maintaining are virtually nothing in the scheme of this. If
    you don't let me eat the way I want to, without judgment, I
    end up eating ridiculously. I know you don't trust me—don't
    deny this, I know you don't; no one could after last year—so
    you'll just have to understand that I don't want to sacrifice
    university next year and that I'm trying to take care of myself.
    You can't protect me for the rest of my life. The first time I
    leave home I probably will fall back into the familiar behavior,
    but I'll get myself out of it. Because there's too much that I
    want to do with my life to let myself wallow in it.

7. *If you attack me, I get defensive. The anorexic voices wheedle*
    their way into my brain and tell me that the family would
    be better off without me. THIS IS NOT EMOTIONAL
    BLACKMAIL, if you're thinking that right now, Dad. That
    is the way it is, and if you think I am playing you, then it is
    only further evidence of your ignorance in relation to how this
    nightmarish disorder works. It plays with my mind. Sometimes
    when I speak it is not entirely me. It is my anorexic self. I don't
    expect either of you to understand this. When you get angry
    with me, I get a strong urge to retreat back into the familiar
    behaviors of the eating disorder. Because "it" understands me,
    and "it" doesn't judge. "It" comforts me and doesn't threaten.

8. *The Internet forums I contribute to are very important to me.*
    They are full of girls who are going, and have been through,
    the same things that I have. They understand, like no one else
    can. I mentioned that I keep an online journal. Those girls

on my forum are free to look and comment in it. I am free to comment in theirs. We all help each other and try to remind each other that life beyond the eating disorder is possible. I have one particular friend who is getting worse and is very much in the thick of it. She distresses me, but I'm helping her. Through helping her, I'm indirectly helping myself. I helped another girl up to the stage where I'm at now and we share a really close bond because we both understand what the other has been through.

9. Anorexia isn't all about "attention." Or emotional blackmail. Or dramatic wheedling. It took virtually everything from me, and I'm only just starting to recover bits back. It is not something I revel in. I hate it passionately. Nothing makes me angrier than to see another girl submitting slowly to this blackness. But as I said, it is a perverse addiction and holds on to you very tightly.

10. It's not a case of university versus anorexia. That's such a simplistic way of looking at it. I'm not trying to deliberately sabotage my life. I mean, come on. I never meant to do that. Anorexia latches on, lies to you, and makes you believe that it is your true identity, your true calling. You may scoff. Again...you can't understand. Anorexia steals your "self." And to claim your original self back, you have to execute this anorexic self you've come to feel secure in. That's hard.

11. This isn't a game. And if it is...it is not one I'm particularly enjoying playing.

12. This isn't about weight, or a diet or a figure. Somewhere along the line, I've come to equate fat with failure and weakness. Weight loss is merely symptomatic of the greater psychological problem.

13. Anorexia expresses a deep personal inadequacy...a difficulty in adjusting to your place in the world...an inability to feel that you can ever be good enough. I wanted to disappear. I wanted to be desperately sick. To show myself, and you, that I was scared (of expectations, of life) and just needed to slow

down. I did have holes. I wanted to feel vulnerable. I can't do everything. I'm not bloody perfect. I wanted to whittle all the shit away from me and expose my true self. I also wanted to avoid myself and my chances. I didn't want to have to make decisions. I wanted to escape.

14. *I just want you to leave me alone. Stop the accusations of emotional blackmail, stop trying to force-feed me, stop the comments about my erratic eating, and stop the odd glances when I eat at weird times. Stop the assumption that all of this is my fault and I could snap out of it if I wanted. Stop seeing anorexia in the light of traditional studies that assume it is about either a) attention, b) domineering parents, or c) avoiding sexuality. Because for me, it is about none of those. Stop being overprotective. Let me learn and deal with myself. I love you and I need you to just let me be. If I can't feel comfortable and understood in my own family, then where on earth can I?*

15. *Please understand that this whole thing has been a profoundly altering experience. It isn't over yet. I probably will fall back into it at points during my life. I don't believe it is possible to recover 100 percent. I am not who you used to think I was. You can't pretend I'm the same person. I feel so radically different from the old Lucy. I've swum out too far and, as of yet, I'm resisting the shore. Just give me a break and realize that I don't want to self-destruct anymore. There's too much that I want to live for. I'm just trapped. Not as much as I used to be, though. This is an awful cycle that gets faster and faster...and almost falls apart spinning off in every direction. It has only just started to slow down in me. But it's still moving.*

16. *All I need you to do is...SUPPORT ME. That's it. That's all you can do. You can't magically erase last year and magically erase this disorder. You can't make it all better, and I wouldn't want you to anyway. As hard as it may be to accept, you literally cannot do anything. That's why so many people with loving families die of this. You need to trust that I don't want to be like this forever and that I will hoist myself out of it in time. I just need you to be there for me, nonjudgmental,*

unconditional, always. Let me fix myself up. This is an independent, isolating, and solitary disease. You can't help me if I don't want to help myself. I am the only person who can make me better. If you could just support me and be there for me...that's all I could want.

• • •

Anorexia has taken:

- *my identity*
- *my parents' trust in me*
- *my trust in myself*
- *my friends*
- *my chance to be at the top of my class*
- *my chance to do well in all of my subjects*
- *my dream of a near perfect mark in the HSC*
- *my confidence*
- *my ability to feel "good enough"*
- *my naiveté*
- *my brain*
- *my dream to apply to Oxford*
- *my motivation to do anything*
- *my dream to go away to London after school*
- *my independence*
- *my pride*
- *my self-esteem*
- *my ability to think*
- *my health*
- *my laughter*
- *my height*
- *my self-sufficiency*
- *my dignity*

- *my energy*
- *my honesty*
- *my self-respect*
- *my hair*
- *my freedom*
- *my emotions*
- *my tolerance*
- *my control*

In short, my life and soul. But I'm getting it back. Bit by agonizing bit.

• • •

I laughed for the first time a few weeks ago. It was amazing. I had never even missed it. Mum and my brother immediately stopped talking and looked at me. The silence was palpable. And all I could remember thinking? *Oh shit. I must be fat.*

Take that for twisted anorexic thought.

• • •

Awful day.

I don't know what's wrong with me. I think I might be going mad.

I am lonely...I feel deserted and rejected. I also feel like a heffalump, but I know that can't be true because I made one of my friends cry yesterday over how I still looked like "skin and bone." Good thing she didn't see me a few months ago.

I've spent most of the afternoon feeling sorry for myself, upstairs, sitting in a corner, crying. And then I had a little sleep where I imagined I was taking lots of pills...so I called my aforementioned friend and cried on the phone to her. I felt like such an idiot. I hate exposing weakness.

I haven't eaten much today. And I only ate breakfast yesterday. I simply don't want to. And I'm not going to eat if I'm not hungry. And besides, I had four glasses of champagne last night and it must have calories.

The voices are coming back.

• • •

I should walk around with this sign strapped to my forehead which says:

I am...

- boring
- inclined to hyperactivity when nervous
- inclined to speak very quickly when nervous
- inclined to say stupid things spontaneously without realizing the consequences

It would make everything much easier. Then maybe I wouldn't disappoint so many potential friends when they find out that the content is not so colorful as the pretense.

• • •

I met my friend A through an anorexia forum on the Internet. We have decided to meet up. Before I leave, I want to send her an e-mail, though. I'm scared she'll be so disappointed in me.

To: A
From: Lucy

Okay, A, I hope you read this before we meet up today. Actually, on second thoughts, it would be better if you didn't because this exposes me for the horribly insecure and idiotic person I am..

1. I'm terrified you'll see me and think I'm fat and then go home and not want to talk to me because I'm not a real anorectic.

2. When I'm shy and nervous I tend to clam up a bit—please don't think I'm boring and have nothing to say!

• • •

THE GRAND STORY OF LUCY AND A'S MEETING IN THE CITY

1. Lucy almost gets arrested (minimal exaggeration employed for dramatic effect) on the bus for paying the wrong fare. Luckily the evil policeman with brown teeth took pity by virtue of her saccharinely apologetic smile.

2. *Meanwhile, A sits on steps of Town Hall.*

3. *Late (as usual), Lucy hurries through city trying to juggle bag, mobile, and iPod, trying to look effortlessly cool, whilst holding stomach in to appear thinner.*

4. *Lucy sees A. How does she know it is her? A is very thin and has blonde hair…and that "anorexics anonymous" vibe.*

5. *Lucy and A trot off to get some coffee. A buys a cappuccino. Lucy buys a flat white. She was going to get a small one, but as A was getting a regular-sized coffee, she got a regular one too, so it didn't feel like they were competing or something.*

6. *Sitting on a bench in Hyde Park, they are accosted by an almost toothless man with an Eastern-European accent and purple jumper who proceeds to tell them why smiling is so important as it makes the world beautiful. He pulls out a sleek little pencil case. Green tartan. Lucy is convinced he would now pull out a little silver gun and shoot them both at close range. Instead, he takes out little slips of paper printed with quotes and donates them to Lucy over the period of half an hour. Luckily, they escape just as Lucy's patience snaps.*

7. *A and Lucy are accosted again, this time by a busload of Asian tourists. They request photos, and after deciding that they probably were not touring as part of an international pedophile/pornographer/indecent-voyeur clique, the blonde-anorexics-anonymous had their photo taken with two of them, who were very excited and very balding.*

• • •

I am currently eating a marzipan, sultana, and rum-filled white chocolate and hating every second of it. I'm such a disgusting, piggish, gross, flabby shithead.

However, if it could be guaranteed that I could eat whatever I wanted without putting on weight, I'd have warm mashed potato with butter and chives, lightly crisped pancakes with maple syrup, a crème brûlée with raspberries, sticky date pudding with really thick butterscotch sauce, a plate of pumpkin risotto, roasted pumpkin (blackened), slices and slices of grilled and seasoned Halloumi cheese, some Bircher muesli with natural yogurt, Siena cake/panforte studded with nuts and black gooeyness, croissants with French cherry jam, a Swiss potato rösti (golden and crispy), an Indian coconut and potato curry, Chinese fried rice, a caramel latte with cinnamon and lots of froth, and a toffee apple.

Oh, and a good lemon curd tart.

And those smashed broad beans with olive oil and pecorino cheese I had in Italy.

And roasted rhubarb with homemade custard.

And a proper apple crumble with a little dollop of vanilla bean ice cream…

And a whole pot of homemade brandy butter—by itself.

And a warm raspberry and white chocolate brownie…with fudgy sauce.

And pesto pasta, or pesto on a pizza base, or pesto on cheese, or pesto with anything, really. I could even do a repeat of that lovely binge where I ate the pesto straight from the jar. No spoon necessary. And finished it.

• • •

Bones. At the end of the day, they will not change. I have my own frame and no starving or bingeing can change that. I'll always have my wide hips, simply because no matter how much fat I lose, I can't shrink bone. I have a fixed shape. *So there, anorexia.* I used to think that maybe I could make them smaller in some way by losing weight; that I could just wither and fade to the point of *nothingness.* Let's not get caught up in the biologically ugly death by starvation. The desire isn't always to die: it's to disappear. That's different. But bones don't burn away like flesh does.

My body is unique…I can lose and gain as much weight as I want *but the bones will still be exactly the same.*

I find that comforting.

So I guess the only thing there is for me to do is to nurture my body as well as I can, because it's the only one I'll ever have and there's no point torturing myself.

I mean, where's the point to that? I have a freaking life to live and too much that I want to do and achieve.

I guess I'm just trying to justify the nachos I had for dinner. But seriously, I'm sick of spending my brain's limited energy on calories and whether I can have a smear of avocado on my rice cracker or not.

The idea of health is also peculiar. I threw myself into starvation "for health"—to peel away the layers of unhealthy and dirty fat. Now I'm forcing my reasoning to change. A little fat is good…just enough to cover the crevices and cushion the muscles and bones, and fill out my chest and cheeks…just enough to be healthy. I'm forcing myself to recognize that the withered human form of protruding bones and gaps and spaces is not what I want and *is not healthy*. Is not attractive. Is not sustainable.

• • •

I wish someone would smite all of the cereal and crumpets in the world and replace them with friendly chunks of pineapple and mango.

I feel sick.

Tired.

Anorexia-nostalgic.

Sad.

Empty.

Lonely.

Useless.

• • •

I think in some strange way I've never connected myself emotionally with "That Girl in the Mirror." I watched her curiously as she got thinner and thinner, but when I looked at myself I saw fat. I could feel it, point to it, hold it.

"But that's just skin!" Mum would plead.

Skin or not, it was fat. Eff Aay Tee. Fat. Anything attached to me was unnecessary and had to be gotten rid of. Otherwise, for all the excess, I'd never be able to find a new, exciting Lucy.

Sometimes, when I looked in the mirror, I would feel my peripheral vision fade to focus purely on that flat, glassed portrait. And I'd feel my "self" melt away. I have stood in front of the mirror for over half an hour, unable to unfix my eyes. The portrait of a girl diseased, but not me.

●　●　●

I feel very dark.

I know something's up when I can hardly move for utter exhaustion, and I try to avoid walking the dog.

Down.

Triggered, probably, by going shopping for an hour this afternoon. I tried on a pair of expensive jeans and they didn't fit. I thought nothing of it because I realized I'd picked out my anorexic size, not my new, semi-recovered one. The saleswoman, a petite woman with brown hair and gauzy eyes, came over and asked me how I had got on. I said that they just didn't "work"; a reasonable answer, I thought. Sometimes jeans just don't work, dammit. She then wanted to know why.

Ahh. You're one of those, I thought. I flipped my hair and mirrored her stance. She shifted.

"You know how jeans just don't sit right sometimes?" I said.

Pause.

"Is it because they're skinny-leg jeans?" she asked.

Whoops. There went my self-esteem. Flop and splat in the middle of the changing-room floor. I smiled an ersatz smile.

"Probably."

She looked at me sympathetically. I could have biffed her.

I have fucking enormous legs. It doesn't matter how many bones I can count on my torso, my thighs always stay the same. Chunky. Loose.

I'm a fucking loser. A stupid bloody failure. I'm never going to get out of this because I don't want to. I'm so fucking sick of myself. I just want to starve myself into oblivion—translate my self-hatred into something tangible. I want to waste away into absolutely nothing and never have to *feel* anything again. It's not about the weight. It's *not* about the weight. The thing is, the weight comes to symbolize the greater problem. The weight becomes the adopted nexus of the issue. Because it, at least, can be constrained. And a starving body is a wonderful distraction from any of the real, underlying issues. Let's all pretend it's solely about weight and vanity and leave those sore bits alone.

I just want to get rid of myself. Because, let's face it: I'm never going to get anywhere. I'm going to spend my whole life battling this recovery shit. I wish I could just fade into the air, into space, into the sky, into the pavement and go...without anyone noticing. I don't want to die. I just want...to cease to exist in a bodily fashion. I just want to dissolve into transparency.

I've failed. I'm a failed anorectic and a failed recoverer. I can't help people because I'm just a fucking hypocrite who can't do it herself.

But listen to yourself, Luce. A "failed anorectic"? Tell me what the hell a successful anorectic is. Is a successful anorectic that emaciated skeleton dying of heart failure? Hairless, colorless, emotionless, and soon-to-be lifeless? Is that your idea of success?

How is it possible to "fail" at anorexia?

Oh yes, I'm a failure because I'm not being intravenously fed and haven't died of a heart attack yet.

I think I'd prefer to fail at something a little more worthwhile. Or at least something that doesn't cite "death" as its only success.

I wonder if you can be a "failed" cancer patient? *"Oh shit, my cancer hasn't spread to my bones/liver/blood/remaining organs. My pubic hair and eyelashes haven't all fallen out. Why can't I just...get there?"*

Umm...and where was that, again?

• • •

Life is an odd thing. We are so, so, so, so, so, so, so incredibly miniscule, almost meaningless, in the overall scheme of *eternity*. Calories don't even register.

I think I'm losing weight again. Albeit indirectly. It's not a conscious decision, but more along the lines of not *needing* three prunes for breakfast, so only having two...or not *needing* a sandwich for lunch, so having an icy pole and an apple instead...of not *needing* to drink cordial or fruit juice because water's just fine…I feel strangely passionless about the whole thing. I mean, I could not do it, but somehow it's easier to just sit back and watch.

. . .

Something I thought would never happen has happened.

My future self, take note: I binged on All-Bran.

Possibly the most disgusting, dry, flaky cereal in the world. Only mildly palatable when soaked in milk or combined with some other cereal and eaten with banana, warm. But this time *I ate it by itself.* (Insert dramatic shudder.)

It was really hot today. On the bus home there was no air conditioning. I honestly thought I would melt into a hot puddle and slosh around on the floor. Serious heat. Over forty degrees Celsius. I'm talking being able to feel sweat dribble down your back and having your jeans melt into the plastic seating so that there's this great "unsticking" noise when you stand up. I was so anxious about this I stood up in increments: I put a little weight on my feet, waited a few minutes, rose up a little more, waited a second, then a bit more…so as to save myself from the sweaty ripping "stuck jeans" orchestra which is so mortifying.

. . .

Today I went to the dentist. I voluntarily told him about my eating disorder. I was worried that my purging may have affected my teeth.

He said, "You don't look like there's anything wrong with you!" This was accompanied by a hearty slap on the back and a fatherly (read patronizing "oh-you-silly-girl") smile.

"I ate my way out of anorexia. That's what you do, isn't it? Ha, ha, ha."

Oh yes. Chortle, chortle indeed.

I gave him a withering smile and opened my mouth.

"Oh," he said. *"Will you look at those receding gums!"*

Ha. Ha. Ha.

A few months ago after an incident like this, I wouldn't have eaten for the next week. Today I just couldn't be bothered.

. . .

I feel like rolling around in self-disgust. I have eaten:

- *half a packet of soy crisps (fried in sunflower oil)*
- *a pancake with maple syrup*
- *a Curly Wurly bar*
- *a muesli bar*
- *Special K. Always Special K*
- *half a packet of Soho biscuits...nacho flavor*
- *a few seaweed crackers*
- *some random bits of fruit to make me feel better about myself*

And *that* was for afternoon tea. I am numb with misery. I feel so heavy.

. . .

My dietician told me I was obviously no longer "critical" today. That must mean I'm fat.

Shit.

Or I could just be logical about it. *No, you're no longer emaciated. You're "just" scarily thin.* The bizarre thing is that now I've disposed of the "fat" thought, I suddenly feel perversely jealous of how I used to be. Sometimes I wish I had been forcibly removed to hospital instead of having my hysterics humored. It would have made me sickly proud.

. . .

I'm trying to work out who I am.

And it's tedious and upsetting and tender.

Being caught between anorexia and recovery is a weird thing.

It's like being in limbo. I can't be one fully and can't seem to be the other fully.

I feel like I'm waiting for me to swing either way. But part of me doesn't want to commit to either extremity and dangles here, halfway in between.

I'm not succeeding with either because they both tussle with each other equally.

I've never really contemplated being in this state for a long time.

. . .

My psychiatrist has told me to try to engage with the negative/disordered thinking and talk back to it. I thought it was a pretty silly idea. I mean, having conversations with the voices in my head doesn't seem to me to be the greatest sanity-inducing exercise. But I'll give it a go.

When I put on weight, I'll be fat.

a) I will not be fat. b) There is a big difference between emaciation and fatness. Like…a hundred kilograms of difference?

It makes me feel…special.

Ugh. Can't I be special for something else a tad more rewarding?

It makes me feel…in control and strong.

I'm always in control. No one can force me to do anything. And wanting to be in control of life, to the extent of death? Maybe I should try to be in control of my health. More strength is involved in battling this than in giving in to it.

It comforts me.

Most people go for the hot chocolate, marshmallows, and shallow movie option. Self-destruction isn't a bloody comfort. In fact…it's weakness. It's a way to avoid the world instead of standing up and fighting it.

But why do I cling to this? What's it all about?

Have you ever seen a happy anorectic?

. . .

I just stood there eating a bread roll while Dad shouted at me.

I smushed it up into little flat pieces and ate it without even tasting it. My jaws are sore from constantly chewing gum.

Then he strode away and I heard him whispering angrily to Mum in the lounge room, about my selfishness and how I was emotionally "dominating" the family.

I heard everything. So I came out and told him. *"It's not my fucking choice to be like this. It's a compulsion."* He scoffed and challenged me.

I tried to hold strong to my argument but failed, bursting into hot tears.

. . .

I stood at the kitchen sink eating. And eating. And eating. First, a bowl of cereal. Then a plate of dry cereal. Cashews. Handfuls of them. Yogurt. Tortillas. I finished the packet. A bread roll. Pesto from the tub. Cream cheese from the tub. Olives. A packet of Indian spicy mashed potato with peas.

When this happens, I just go blank. Thoughts stop. I gag any protestations with more food. I grip the cupboard doors tightly. Stop for a second. Breathe. Start up again.

I am officially disgusting. Utterly foul.

And fat. Heavy, corpulent, f. a. t.

The anorexia's hissing: *Failure!*

. . .

Christmas in Tamworth, with my Grandma, the old lemon tree, and yellow grass. Here are some sparkling highlights:

- *Grandma saying that I looked great* (I must be fat), *but clearly lying* (I'm still thin, then?!).

- *A Christmas guest who said she "would never have guessed" I'd ever had anorexia* (Oh my God, I must be enormous).

- *Grandma trying to force-feed me the whole time* (… I thought I was fat?), *before catching me accidentally knocking my collarbones painfully against an edge and saying that they really should be covered up* (I'm gross).

- *Going to the bathroom immediately after the vile Christmas lunch and being accused of vomiting.*

- *My intense desire to do the above—a desire that could not be acted upon due to the central location of the bathroom.*

- *My intense desire to exercise—a desire left hanging nervously thanks to incredible heat.*

- *The food. Iceberg lettuce, mayonnaise, beetroot from a can, potato salad from a box, sliced white bread, some poor pig and*

turkey cut and roasted, coleslaw, and water that tasted like the
runoff from a dirt track.

I really am ungrateful. I'm just…so tired.

• • •

I stared at the toilet roll. Do I really want to do this?
You'd be stupid not to since everyone's out of the house.
Mmm.

I set myself up perfectly: towel folded for my knees on the floor,
glass of water by the sink, mouthwash at hand. I washed my hands.
Knelt for a while looking into the toilet bowl and watched a drop of
water stretch…and plop.
I'm not sure I should be doing this. University. My life.
Those tortillas. The Indian.
I stuck my fingers down my throat and purged.
Gross.
Indian food is not fun to purge. Spices hurt the second time
round.

I finished, or rather chickened out prematurely, when I thought
of stomach ruptures.

Wiped my hands with toilet paper. Flushed the toilet. Twice.

Looked at myself in the mirror. Eyes slightly red. Highly unro-
mantic situation made worse by remnants of orange potato strewn
across my cheek. Coughed and tried to dislodge the crap stuck in
my throat.

Drank water. Cleaned my mouth out.
Everyone's still out.
My fingers still smell.
Tears are slipping down my cheeks, but my head is so still.

• • •

It's funny how I used to lie a lot in primary school because I didn't
think people would like me otherwise. I wasn't good enough as I was,
you see. Here are some of the more spectacular lies I told:

- *My mum was our suburb Mayor (which she was, actually),*
  so I told girls I didn't like that they had to be nice to me, or
  otherwise she would put them in jail. This worked a treat.

- *I fooled everyone in my class (we were all very young) into believing I was an angel who could summon and control the wind. I would stand at the head of the playground, waving my arms about spectacularly and muttering unintelligible words beneath my breath.*

- *One day I told my teacher that I would be in a wheelchair the next day as I was very sick. Friends were all duly concerned. I limped home. Asked Mum where I could get a wheelchair from. Considered asking the disabled lady across the road. Needless to say, plan failed.*

- *I was "sick" and away from school for seven weeks when I was eleven with a "mysterious illness" that saw me being carted off to specialists everywhere. They couldn't work out what I had. I'd have these awful night sweats (i.e. get water bottle, unscrew lid, apply liberally). I was found out and sobbed into my Snoopy under my quilt. All I can remember now was Mum and Dad upbraiding me for causing them so much washing.*

- *I pretended to be beaten up by a girl I didn't like, to get her expelled. She wasn't expelled.*

- *I brought an elaborately painted vase in for show and tell in year 2 and told everyone that I'd painted it whilst on holiday in southern France. My teacher didn't believe me and called me a "show-off." I proceeded to "run away" from school and hid in the bathrooms. From where she dragged me an hour later.*

- *I told everyone I was born in Polynesia. The one issue I always had trouble explaining was my extreme paleness. I said that it was the Polynesian habit of young girls to stay in their twig houses until they were at least twelve.*

I make up for all the lying now by being excruciatingly honest. Cringingly open with some people.

My longest lie, of course, only ended a few months ago. I finally got rid of the always-happy-Lucy-who-giggled-and-made-a-fool-of-herself-all-the-time-and-was-never-angry-or-sad-and-made-silly-faces facade that I maintained at school from year 6 to year 12. Was that impressive?

No. Exhausting.

. . .

They are delicately crisp and brown on the outside and stay soft and egg-y on the inside. I pick the pumpkin flowers from the garden and wash them carefully. After cutting off the hairy sepal and nectary, twirl them thick through a batter of egg, flour, and salt, and lie them head-to-toe in a heavily oiled frying pan. I smell them and my neighbor flips them. They crackle. I devour them still hot and glistening gold, trying to ignore the oil.

But now I feel like a flubby lump. Actually, not even a lump. More of a water bomb going splat in slow motion.

. . .

I got into Arts/Law at Sydney University. I just casually slipped this piece of information into a conversation with Mum. I think she said, "Oh thank God."

I'm ecstatic.

Terrified.

And heartbroken. *I don't think I can do it.*

. . .

This morning I stepped on the scales. I had lost two kilograms from the weight I had been half-heartedly maintaining for six months.

And then it dawned on me: my brain was slowing down again.

I realized that I had been slowly cutting back on food for weeks. I had whittled my breakfast down to only low-calorie cereals and half a banana. I was not eating dinner. I was overriding my appetite again. The alarm bells started ringing yesterday when I realized that I *just wasn't hungry.* I wasn't hungry today either. This is what I used to be like in the beginning: *just not hungry.*

Another warning sign is when I can see myself getting bigger and bigger despite the scales. I am withdrawing again. I don't like going out. I hate getting dressed because I don't want my body on show and hate the feeling of clothing against my skin. I am lying about meals again. I am chewing gum and spitting out food again. I have experimented with flavored water as a meal replacement.

I am slipping back. Again.

I MUST NOT LET THIS DESTROY THIS YEAR AS WELL.

So then I broke almost every fucking rule. At 10:04 p.m.

I just binged.

In fact, I'm typing this halfway through a bowl of Apple and Cinnamon Crunchola and natural yogurt. This is after the Indian leftovers, cereal, and cheese.

Here are the rules (the ones that apply to this situation, anyway):

- *The "no cheese slices after lunch" rule.*

- *The "no Indian/fast food leftovers whatsoever" rule.*

- *The "I will never eat full-cream yogurt again" rule.*

- *The "I will not eat Crunchola by itself, but must dilute it with a low-cal cereal" rule.*

- *The "eat at six o'clock, but nothing to be eaten later than seven o'clock" rule.*

Wow, I have never really articulated any of "the rules" before. I have only ever understood them, *felt them*, to be deeply necessary.

• • •

I got up this morning after my binge and crept into the bathroom preparing myself for a massive expansion. I scrutinized my body in the mirror. Oh shit. The thighs. They are so much bigger than yesterday. I squished my arm against my side, so the flesh would spread, and stuck my stomach out. Look at that little fat girl. Stocky. Stodgy. I almost died. And I felt awful because I know that this time I can't do anything about it. I simply cannot afford to let myself into this again. I have to fight it with all that I have. Or I can say goodbye to everything this time.

I went downstairs and stepped on the scales. It took me a few minutes of staring searchingly at the ceiling before I was prepared to look down at the number.

It hadn't gone up. At all.

A big sigh of relief...then momentary panic...then I laughed at myself: my thighs couldn't be bigger if I weighed the same as yesterday.

But they are. Your fat has just redistributed itself overnight, that's all.

Ahh. The little anorexic niche of my brain always has an answer on hand. But really…no, hang on, that's ridiculous.

. . .

"Fat" is just a feeling, so it has no relevance to reality whatsoever. As my psychiatrist would explain to a hysterically defiant me, time and time again, you can't feel fat. It's a physical substance, not a mental state. The idea of "feeling fat" is just symbolic of the underlying feelings.

I finally realized what I was feeling: unmanageable, bloated, queasy, confused, fearful, worthless, unhappy, distended, and lonely. And somehow my brain translated all that into one easy word: FAT.

Just like my brain had superimposed all the darker issues upon each other, and labeled the stack: WEIGHT.

Worry about weight. Not social inadequacy. *Anorexia: A wonderful way to calcify all your problems without touching them once!*

It took me a while to believe her, needless to say.

. . .

Weight?

When I was really ill, life for a while resembled something similar to the Theatre of the Absurd…meaningless…desperate…futile. I was searching for something. Anything. Now it's more like a farce, revolving around something so incredibly trivial. Half of my brain is embarrassed to think what the other half does. Am I really that vain?

But I guess we, of all people, know that it isn't about vanity, is it?

I have no memories of those black months. They were thick. I only remember not wearing seatbelts in cars…just in case we crashed…walking across roads without looking and willing a bus to come speeding around the corner…investigating my oven for its gassing-capabilities, lying on my bed sweating and writhing with terror when I first felt the blackness come over me.

And I remember the overriding despair and futility. The exhausted tears.

If I lie on my side, all my flesh falls away and I can hold my hipbone again with my whole hand...it's comforting. Empty spaces are just so simple.

. . .

It's nice when, for one moment, I realize that maybe the past six months of agonized recovery-poking may not have been as futile as I first thought. When I finally realize that the stultifying shyness and social avoidance the anorexia necessitated may be lessening, that my brain is oiling its cogs and squeaking, that I can let myself connect with someone I would have hidden from half a year prior. When I finally realize that I am finding myself again; that I've stepped forward; that I am learning to live and breathe again.

And when all of this is prompted by one person, within the space of four hours, I realize just how effectively I have been blinding myself.

He was lovely.

. . .

My dreams scare and thrill me.
There are too many of them and not enough time.
And I'm so small...I mean nothing.

. . .

Those conflicting desires of the anorectic to be seen simultaneously as fragile and flimsy and autonomous and controlled.

There's a seed of a good feminist debate in there...desiring both the image of weakness and of strength...I've come to the conclusion that everyone is just a cluster of paradoxes and differing degrees of contradiction. Perhaps an eating disorder is the biggest contradiction of all.

But being a damsel really is a bit of a bore. Excuse me, but I refuse to be "saved" by anyone but myself.

I don't like being pitied. I'd like to believe that, anyway.

. . .

Reading *Wasted* last night, I had this deep, painful, irrepressible urge to go backward. Then I realized that I've effectively wasted my opportunity. University starts in two months. And next holidays, I'll be in Europe and to restrict food in Switzerland is criminal. So when? When can I do it?

I fell asleep.

This morning I still feel slightly mad and the urge is still ringing. I want to be morbidly fragile...vulnerable...breakable. I want my friends to visit me and think with a thrill of horror: *"Oh fuck. She's so thin."*

. . .

You didn't go far enough. You could have gone so much further.

Could I have?

You didn't need to get better. How could you get better if there was nothing really wrong with you?

I was sick, you deadshit.

I'm terrified about university.

Yes. And there's a very easy way to escape that. It's safe...it'll give you something to do. And you won't have to worry about anything.

I can't. I can't let myself do that again. I would never forgive myself.

So what sort of BMI reading is that? Come on, you can do better. And maybe this is all you're here for anyway? To waste away and die in some hospital bed? Slow suicide is preferable. Gives you a while to get used to the idea.

God, I hate this.

You can't recover when you were never sick in the first place.

Everyone else thought I was.

Yeah? And they were fat.

Fuck it. Fuck the stupid fucking brain and fucking, stupid, damn, crappy thing.

I can't seem to psychologically adjust myself to being this weight. I can see fat in places where it wasn't before, I'm sure. *Unless maybe I'm seeing my body properly now for the first time? And I was always fat?*

Oh come on, that really is ridiculous. What a load of shit you're talking.

• • •

The phone rang today. I picked up grudgingly. There was an English-sounding guy on the other end.

"Hullo there, I was wondering if I could speak with Mr. Taylor?"

"No, sorry, he isn't here at the moment...okay. Thanks...bye."

English. And then I remembered that I wanted to go to London.

Silly things keep you going don't they?

London. The moment I touch down someday will be one of those wonderfully anticlimactic moments when you look forward to something for so, so, so long and then—finally—it happens. And that's that.

You're still *you*.

Despite the change of scene, the new cast, it's still you sweating behind the mask.

The Darkness Is Sulking

The darkness is sulking.
I poke it with my pen.
It cringes and crawls into a corner
Leaving greasy gray footprints.
Letters cuddle the nib and glue as one
Into crooked meaning:
Lone words
That dissolve in leaden circles
Lob into shadow and seldom return.

But
Sometimes,

         ...they do.

Another jab,
Another prod,
Another wheezing pink pit.
A stab in the back
A blinding fissure in black–

...I win.

. . .

Maybe we should stop focusing on starving ourselves and start focusing on developing some super-duper plan to hijack all the world's nuclear power plans and use the money fed into them for feeding and clothing the poor of the world.

Yeah. That's it.

And maybe we should stop giving birth to a quarter of a million babies each day and start giving loving homes to those kids who don't have one at all.

I always think too much when I'm bored. Bad habit. I keep forgetting that you're not supposed to think.

. . .

I know something's up when all I can do is listen to melancholic Coldplay songs and stare at nothing in particular.

The combination of late medication and looking up suicide on the Internet at midnight really shouldn't be mixed. And no, I'm not going anywhere. It just morbidly fascinates me.

. . .

I forget sometimes about the funeral. I forget sometimes that she was killed at all. The knowledge of it is too shuddering…too loud. She was seventeen; that is ghastly and premature. Painfully freakish. Fateful. But yet, it really happened. And it really happened over a year ago, now.

I was at the funeral; everyone was. It was blisteringly hot as February always is in Sydney. Heading toward my lowest weight, I was bones beneath my uniform. The girl next to me fainted. I helped carry her outside. Went back inside. Couldn't cry. As the white coffin crept down the aisle, I wanted to run out in front of all the pale audience; to laugh and scream, "No, it's alright, this isn't actually happening, it's all pretend!'

The sounds her mother made—low, scratched, wrenchingly exorcised, the animalistic sobs she tore from her heart—couldn't even convince me. And now, so much later, I still cannot believe. That it is I who lived; despite tiptoeing along the edge of death; despite contemplating the descent, the end, coming so close; and yet she, she, was taken: in a fraction of a second.

I breathe—as she should be—and remember why I hadn't gone on that camp where she was killed.

I was too sick. An excuse I scoffed at but silently welcomed.

Leaving the funeral, I remember blurred people looking at me. I held tightly on to my wrists. The only face I remember was of a boy, who I had danced with six years earlier at a school barn dance. Staring. Sadly? I held my stomach in and tried to make myself look thinner. Never mind the sinewy neck; never mind the wasted calves; the school blazer *might*—God forbid—make me look fat; *make me look normal, whole. Belie the broken.*

. . .

I realized today that I have this innate difficulty understanding why anyone would like *me*. Fuel for the flames of bloody paranoia.

Maybe the connection I feel to this person is purely platonic and imagined. I'm moving too fast. Trying to swallow up this tasty new life before I should. I'm new to this relationship game. I've never done it before. I probably should have let a stable friendship form before I jump in the deep end and expose myself. But something is making my stomach fizz and head spin, lately. I feel like I'm on the very crest of something thrilling. And what if I miss it?

. . .

The plums are good this time of year. Plump and firmly squishy. I split the smooth skin with a knife...watch the beads of juice gather on the breadboard...gaze at the plush redness inside.

. . .

Please excuse the fucking swearing. I'm just so fucking sick of this whole thing. If I'm going to be a fucked-up social failure, I'd at least prefer to be an *emaciated* fucked-up social failure.

Fuck the whole fucking, stupid, damn, fucking thing. I hate it. No, sorry, rephrase: how about, *I hate me.*

Fuck it, fuck it, fuck it, fuck it. I'm just so insipid. Flaccid.

Come on, girl! Get some fucking confidence!

Fuck it. No one got to the top of the UN or won a Nobel Prize for Literature by starving themselves.

I have a fucking good figure. I was told that when I was ten kilograms heavier, for God's sake. I want to be known for my brains and social prowess, not my ability to slowly commit suicide.

Look at me! Look at me! I'm killing myself! Aren't you proud? Jealous? Ha ha!

I'm going to exercise and exercise until I melt all this disgusting crap from me. Maybe then I'll find a lovely, confident, socially extroverted Lucy beneath all this emotional residue.

• • •

I'm having another bubble-of-happiness moment.

I honestly don't know what's wrong with me.

I never thought I'd ever feel this way.

I think it's a combination of thinking about a certain person...university almost starting...and joining lots of revolutionary clubs. I have direction...and it isn't a self-destructive road I'm taking this time.

I like my body. Ha. Haven't ever said that one, have I? I got up this morning...stripped down just to my undies, scrutinized...and I could *see it.* And I *like* it. I might even start crying. I *like* it. This is such a foreign, bizarre, mind-twisting concept. How long has it taken for me to get here?

It's moments like these that I'm braving the anguish of recovery for. I had my first one a few days ago.

I have my very dark moments still. But my days are splattered with good moments where I just like *me.* And that's a big change from the endless gray and black that defined my life for too long.

Now I'm very lightly gray. But with pink polka dots.

I believe in recovery right now. I disillusion myself on the days when I curl up and cry and feel awful and lost. But they're counterbalanced with these precious rosy moments.

• • •

Should I ring him?

Or not?

Maybe not. I saw him on Tuesday...and messaged him on Thursday. Today's Friday. That's probably too soon.

I'm supposed to be above this silliness. I'm not meant to like boys...that completely upsets my life plan of living alone and dying alone with three cats and a pig.

Tricky. Shyness can be disabling.

This is agonizing.

. . .

I just sat and ate five hundred cals' worth of Crunchy Nut cereal in one go, over half an hour, whilst watching some crap on TV that involved Brad Pitt with long hair and lots of women impaling themselves on fences. Well, actually, only one: the other one was shot accidentally.

I love midday movies.

I'd love them even more if I didn't feel the need to binge during them.

I'd generally be semi-okay with this binge and just have raw veggies for dinner. But as it is, I'm locked into going out to a Greek restaurant tonight. So now I'm having great fun torturing myself and completing some overdue psychological mutilation.

. . .

I feel wonderfully...*pedestrian*. Not such a fabulous feeling. I'm still trying not to think about that anorexic girl in my Law lectures.

How could I have gotten as thin as I did and not have been able to see what I must have looked like?

So, woo hoo! You almost killed myself! Yeah! Good one Luce! That'll get you far! People will remember you for that! For your nature-defying ability to refuse food! Now that's something worthy of respect!

. . .

I am just so, so, so, so *exhausted*. It almost kills me hauling myself from my bed to sit at the computer. University just tires me out. It takes me an hour to get there and an hour back and the bus ride back is always hot and sticky and full of hot and sticky people. I stand there, try to ignore the sweat on my face and the sweat dripping down the backs of my legs, and try to listen to music, all the while begging my legs not to give up on me.

I could fall in a heap.

. . .

I've put on a kilo.

So after I got off the scales, what did I do? Went out into the kitchen and ate. Cereal, bread rolls, tortillas, gingernut biscuits. Cashews.

And then I just lay on my bed and cried.

. . .

I felt my brain fade. Just slightly. Enough to muddle the words so that all I could do was sit back and stare blankly or lean forward, try to listen, and not understand.

A soft gray settled. Walked out with K. Silent. Hugged K, walked to the bus stop. Silent. Onto the bus.

"A student through to Wynyard, please."

I sit down at the back of the bus across from a very thin boy-man. With floppy curls and a hollowed face. I was attracted, I have to admit. I turned on my iPod. The boy-man unslouched himself and bowled himself from the bus. Loped up the street. Lit a cigarette and kept loping. Yes, I was attracted. Something made me want to scream: *"I'm not really an ignorant and transparent little kid studying Law at Sydney University! I'm a democratic socialist, an agnostic, and I've read Sylvia Plath!"* I didn't, of course. So I went back to listening to music. Changed buses. Sat opposite a man who made me really uncomfortable. He kept looking at me. Up and down with a faint smile on his face. I felt completely and utterly naked. Drew my bag up to my chest, stared the other way. Tried to listen through the gray pall.

Home. Flat, numb, gray; I eat. Go upstairs; lie down. Faintly colorless.

• • •

The first week of university is almost over. While I was rifling through my vegetarian society and Red Cross club papers, the phone rang. I knew who it was.

So we're going to see each other next weekend.

Hendrix. Chocolate. Hugs. Cinnamon pancakes. Perhaps a swim at midnight?

He's going to take me on an acid trip. Then perhaps I'll write a "Kubla Khan."

While on the phone, I turned the light off. Felt the darkness press on me, watched the streetlight across the street. Listened to his voice. We talked about baths. Baths by candlelight. Baths in the dark. Baths with another. Cereal. Touch, sexuality. We talked of beauty, too. The beauty of bodies, curves, skin.

I did hang up with a sweaty sigh of relief, though.

• • •

I wish my heart would stop fluttering. And I wish the squeezing panic would go away. It makes it hard to breathe. I can't go into the city. I just can't do it. I'm semi-panicking, breathless, and blurred.

Panic
Outside, the forget-me-nots smile
As the sun twinkles teasingly through leaves
Patting the water into glittered shards
Of shadow and light.

Inside,
Lips tightened and eyes dark,
She fingers the beads around her neck
And feels her heart rise and fall:
A quickening of breath in and out;
Leaden air closes in on heart and lung.
The air, breathless and gasping
Hovers thickly and squeezes.

Panic's clammy fingers scuttle
From stomach to heart to throat
Grasping and clinging

Pinching and tamping

Cold sweat. Thoughts race and trip
Spinning and skipping in fragmentary
Loops,

Stumbling
Through brilliant white.
Chattering and whirling;
The mind flurries and hums.
Shaking,
And her throbbing head to ground,
She shrinks from whacked and flashing worlds
While outside the forget-me-nots smile;
And shiver in the wind.

• • •

Major dilemma: I have no soymilk left for breakfast tomorrow. This is *big*. Breakfast is my favorite meal of the day, is carried out semi-religiously and is looked forward to from about 5 p.m. the previous afternoon.

• • •

Feeling like THIS is what I stuck with recovery for.

The wellspring of panic that usually swells in my chest hasn't fizzed at all today. And I haven't felt that blank numbness either.

Now...I have this wonderfully warm cocktail of shy joy, excitement, furtive happiness, and hope that just sits nicely behind my ribs...and it doesn't fizz. It bubbles.

And makes me catch my breath.

I can't stop singing. I still remember the first time I laughed and the first time I spontaneously started singing in the shower again after...it all. It took about six months of sluggish and bitter recovery before I started reclaiming parts of myself. Parts of myself I never realized had gone until the hot shock of feeling them again reminded me of how much I'd sacrificed.

. . .

I like buses, I think. Lots of interesting people on the bus. Sitting next to you. Standing across from you. Walking by outside. Enormously fat people who make you wince when they sit next to you and force you to squish yourself into the wall.

I'm in no mood to be politically correct.

I like watching people. I walk through the city for hours just to watch people. When they glance at me, I smile at them. They always look slightly taken aback. Business is devoid of smiles.

. . .

This world is demented. Humanity is demented and dark and beset by sadness and isolation.

All of this is the result of some...*loss*. I don't know what I mean by that. But there's been some loss of idealism, of naïveté, of innocence in our collective psyche.

Modernity has done something to spark this off.

What is it? Why are rates of eating disorders and depression and depression-related disorders continually on the increase? And why are the cases primarily in the Western world?

If that isn't a scream of warning, I don't know what is. *There is something inherently wrong with Western society and the way in which we view the world and ourselves.*

. . .

Today. Legal research in at the Law school. Lawyers...are...all...so ...serious. They make me want to run up to them and start squirting water in their wigs and flashing red, polka-dot undies just to see some sort of emotional reaction. Some sort of human response. Then again, businessmen are worse.

Coffee with two of the girls and a guy from one of my classes...I had a soy cappuccino, which, on top of my nervousness and general excitement, resulted in mania for about three hours. I laughed, hit my elbow, cackled, had them laughing, made too much noise, and disturbed all the other customers. And the waiters. And the barista. Yay. I got their numbers. I feel loved. Yay for making friends with lovely people.

Then I waited outside the Queen Victoria Building for half an hour for a really close friend. Watched the rain and the people. So many bloody pregnant women. Enormous pregnant women. I'm surprised some of them could actually see where they were going.

Plastic girls squealing and trying to look attractive while running (in heels, ridiculously tight jeans, and ridiculously loose tops) through the rain. Greatly amusing. Lots of amusing people. Sometimes I have to hold my breath to stop myself from giggling.

Friend came. I grabbed her and gave her a big squeezy hug. We squealed. We walked all the way to the Rocks and sat in a teeny cafe called La Renaissance. I had a soy mocha…we shared cake…talked about bitches, sex, anorexia, panic attacks, the beauty of the world, trees, boys, homeless people, how we would live in Florence for a year and learn Italian, friends. I tore up a frangipani into weeny, little bits…and I told her how much I loved her.

On my good days I hardly recognize myself. I'm sick of pretending something else. I'm sick of feeling embarrassed by myself. I sat on the bus on the way home, feet cuddling, hands folded. Listened to Goldfrapp. Read some Nietzsche. I looked out the window at this little leaf resting on the road. Thought about the earth sleeping under it all.

A car drove over my little leaf.

So I looked up at the clouds.

• • •

I started using my autumn/winter moisturizing cream again since it's cooling down.

I unscrewed the lid, and took a sniff to make sure if it was still usable.

Bones-and-skin cold hunger dark gray tears beige wrists jumpers hair anger hipbones loneliness frozen faces and trapped eyes scales walking suspicion crunches running-up-and-down-the-hall-endlessly-when-no-one-was-home Special K salad lies gum no-seatbelts-and-walking-in-front-of-buses voices glances no-sleep-and-nightmares fog silence.

In that one tiny semi-millisecond, the entire last year, my darkest days, flashed in and out again in one overwhelming *wham*.

I flinched.

Tried to do it again. Breathed deeply. It wasn't the same.

I don't think I'll use it.

Crisped Air and Navy Shadows
Crisped air and navy shadows
Silent tarmac; an absence of wind.
The tang of a wood fire melts into the viscous perfume
Of a gas stove left unlit. The night seems deceitful;
Reality's veil and the tiptoes of time
Swallowed by sleep.
You shy away
From those streetlights;
So white and so sharp
At odds with the moon.

Kamikaze moths.
And twilight butterflies.
Naked side streets
Lie prostrate until sunrise.
A car–the flash of headlights,
And you look away,
Veer to the left,
See your tail,
Double round,
Stop;
And scratch–
With your foot to ear.

Come on, love.
Wag your way ahead,
Past the winking windows and open doors.

We'll slip through together.

Jumping at shadows, you yelp,
And look up at me,
With those eyes;
With that soul.

• • •

Today I'm more skewed toward negativity. It was all fine and dandy until I saw another anorexic girl at university. Me…but ten kilograms lighter. Hollowed out legs, wrists, red jumper. She looked miserable. If I see her again, I'm going up to her. Not aggressively, just to say something along the lines of "I'm in recovery from anorexia, and I just want you to know that if you ever need someone to talk to, I'm here."

I walked on, acutely conscious of the size of my thighs. Some guy smiled at me.

Oh God, he's smiling because he's laughing inwardly at my fatness compared to that girl.

No, seriously.

Walking to a coffee stand, I had a debate with myself. A long black? Or a flat white?

I went with the long black. Why? *If I'm going to lose weight, I might as well get used to it.*

It was disgusting. I just can't do the proper coffee thing.

I crept into the quadrangle…sat on a sandstone wall…tucked my legs up and under me…and read some of my history reading.

I watched the clouds creep across a puddle…ants…smelt the freshly cut grass (so green and fresh and wet I wanted to eat it—or at least roll around in it) and watched the shadow of a plane cut the clouds.

Then I went back to reading about the de-Christianization and secularization of France during the revolution.

Oh, and I officially have friends. They told me.

• • •

Sometimes I just want to give up.

Or at least allow myself to.

I could reacquaint myself with my bones again…erode my rationality…embrace madness once more…and write poems until I died.

A huddle of bones and gaping spaces. It isn't romantic, but it's so goddamn tempting.

If I write any more, I won't be able to sleep for nostalgia. It's like coming so, so spine-tinglingly, heart-flutteringly close…and then running away.

But coming close to what? Did I want to die?

To be honest…I can't say no. But then again, I can't manage a resounding yes either. I guess I always felt exempt from biology.

It wouldn't happen to me; I'd just be able to get thinner and thinner until I reached some magical, enlightening "end" that wasn't death, exactly, but…

• • •

Let's divert our attention just briefly. Let's consider the current furor over anorexic models. Let's consider the current push for "real-sized" models. Let's consider the newspaper article I read very recently, calling for normal-sized mannequins in shop windows, the banning of thin models at fashion shows, and the projection of a "healthier," more "natural" body shape, so that we may prevent eating disorders. Put simply, I decry the trivialization. Anorexia is not about thin models, nor is it about fashion shows. Both, certainly, can help seed the disease and encourage its continuation. Both, certainly, do nothing to help. These proposed measures are certainly admirable, but I should like to think they are for society's own relief and not touted as the next best recovery strategy for the eating disordered.

"Eating disorders and the media." This has to be one of the most socially self-indulgent, threadbare subjects in the media out there. Generally constructed along the lines of: "This is Barbara. She has been suffering from anorexia for seven years. All around us we see stick-thin models and advertisements for suctioned, highly glossed beauty. Oh dear. When will the media come to terms with the fact that they are killing our teenage girls with pictures?" It's a load of shit. Certainly the media plays a role in furthering anorexia and, indeed, in seeding it in some young people. But it is by no means a major factor. Self-criticism, defeatism, an inability to deal with things; a need to absolve oneself of expectation, of one's SELF in its entirety—*they* are the building blocks.

Biologically, genes perhaps play the greatest role. There is evidence that genes passed through families may predispose people to anorexia (and, I would argue, other similar anxiety disorders). I'm becoming more and more convinced that environment acts as a sort of spark that sets the process in motion but doesn't necessarily initiate it. As does temperament. The most perplexing thing about anorexia is that every case appears to have been hatched by a slightly different meeting of factors and circumstance. There is no set formula. That's what makes me so angry when I see people try to explain it away as born of media saturation or thin models or vanity or even that wonderfully clichéd idea of "control." Certainly these are contributing factors, and in some cases considerably so. But it also takes a deep self-doubt and disgust to starve yourself. To truly, intrinsically believe that eating is superfluous in your case; that eating to maintain your life is somehow presumptuous; that you honestly do not have a being worthwhile enough to warrant preservation through nourishment. This is when it gets tricky, and this is when people like to turn away and blanket the cases with the "let's blame the media" excuse or, worse, "let's blame the mother." I forget how many people have insinuated that my ambitious, intelligent mother was somehow to blame.

It's a psychological no-man's land. I don't profess to have any more of a clue than anyone else. I only have the memory of the nightmare.

• • •

I went for a run in the pouring rain.

In my bikini.

Into the bush and around the lawn and through the flowers and into the lemon tree. The lemons were round and fleshy, dripping.

And I felt free.

(Okay, so I admit it. The whole time I was thinking, *Oh well, this'll burn a few extra calories!*)

• • •

I'm in some sort of swirling cone of hedonism. I'm FEELING so intensely. I think my body is starting to wake up. Walking through the city as rain spat on my shoulders and danced on my eyelashes…my skin after a shower…feeling my little dog's heart thud in his chest…and mine throb in my throat.

Shit holy fucking crap. Where have I been all this time?

If there was ever an argument truer for the dualism of body and soul…mine are just starting to forgive each other.

Law camp was *crazy*. Excuse me while I relate the craziness. Otherwise I'll forget. Alcohol and such.

Very profound moment before I left on the train. I saw that anorexic girl again and something snapped inside me, rather like a rubber band against my heart. I introduced myself. We sat. Exchanged polite chitchat. A bit of silence. Then I plunged in.

"Can I ask you a really personal question? Please…don't take it as rude. I just wanted to say that…[struggle] I'm in recovery for…anorexia…and…depression…and [more struggle] I just…wanted to ask…well, let you know that if you…ever need someone to talk to about anything…I'm here."

Silence. I had hit a nerve. Her eyes welled with tears. Mine did too. She threw herself at me in a desperate hug. It was everything I could do to stop from crying in the middle of Central Station, surrounded by all the other Law students, feeling so intensely connected to this one person, and knowing she felt the same way. I have a feeling that she hadn't admitted it to herself until I asked her. As though it had been hiding at the back of her mind and I had just shone a harsh light on it.

I was, and still am, emotionally wrecked from that one encounter.

Train. Lime-green, fake-leather seats…loud boys…girls. Arrive at Hawkesbury River Station. Am apparently "eye-fucked" by one of the Law Society guys (ha); board a ferry that crashes its way down the river and docks at a primitive wooden wharf.

We assemble in the main hall. Have the customary welcome, introduction, and sexual harassment talk (to raucous laughter).

Find cabins.

Boys take off shirts. Boys play football. Girls sit on grass and watch. Girls twitter. Preliminary drink…fabulous choice between beer or Bacardi Breezers. I can't stand Breezers, so I skull a beer in the toilet. Feel great. Haven't eaten for ten hours.

Dinner consists of lettuce, tomato, cucumber, grated cheese.

An hour later, more drinks. Can't stomach two beers in a row so manage my way through a sickeningly sweet Breezer. Then I grab a beer. And another Breezer. I alternate.

Somebody was calling for volunteers, so I put my hand up. I almost died when I realized it was for a dance-off. I was told to be a banana in a cyclone. Thank God I was semi-drunk. Thank God everyone was semi-drunk and found the whole thing hilariously funny.

Later, I dance. For two hours straight.

K (she is fucking AWESOME, utterly crazy, black hair, red lipstick, attitude, sex appeal) went off in search of reported weed, and there were whispers of cocaine. I feigned shock through my heady haze but secretly wanted to run off and try some.

And really, I'm so naïve. There was a boy. We were dancing together. He asked me if I wanted to go for a walk. Typically, I think: *Yeah! Cool! A walk! I love walks! At night!*

Ten minutes later I was watching myself kissing and rolling around in the grass under the night sky. Who the hell is this person masquerading as Lucy? It felt like I was watching some really awful teen movie. He touched me. He was rough. I told him I really didn't want to do anything because I didn't even know him. We lay there for a while, awkward, my head trying not to touch his shoulder. I couldn't stop thinking about…somebody else. Somehow I managed to convince him to let me go, and we walked back.

I was tired. I switched cabins and ended up sleeping on the wooden floor next to a hole. Woke up early. Went for a walk along the shore with another lovely girl. It was cold. Frosted. Clear. Green and blue. At breakfast there was an intensely awkward moment of eye contact with (or obvious avoidance of) the guy from last night. I looked away nervously and picked at the remaining bits of grass in my hair and stuck to my jumper.

But I had a great time. *Aww. Widdle Wucy's gwowing up.*

• • •

Just a thought: What arrogance to assume sovereignty over all of THIS…the unexplained, the autonomous, the majesty of nature, in which humanity plays such a trivial but destructive role?

• • •

There's something intrinsically wrong with me.

I've been thinking about it.

There's some part of me that I hide…or cover up…or maybe project wrongly.

With all honesty, I can actually say that I don't think anyone can fall in love with me. I don't think I'll ever be in that situation.

I'm too crazy for some people. Too intense for a whole lot more. Too boring. Too serious. Too unhappy or too happy…all at given times. I have too many holes. I'm too vulnerable…and too proud. I'm too everything.

I'm just too much. Either that or…just not…*enough.*

I've been sitting in the lounge room thinking, and sobbing indulgently, about this for the past hour. I never used to care. I've always made excuses. Last year I had no interest anyway. I was dying. Who can be interested in relationships then? I'm just…not right. I make friends with guys…but that's all they want. That's all they ever want.

I manage to royally stuff up any chance I have of being in a relationship by being too shy. Or too manic. Or too…hidden.

I know it sounds absolutely pathetic. *But I just want someone I can go to when the blackness is growling, who'll hold me and love me and not expect anything from me.*

What is so wrong with me?

I haven't cried like this for a while.

Why can't I just be one of those…*normal* girls…you know. The ones who just seem so…*held together.* The ones that people just naturally like. Because they're just…THEM.

I mean, who am I, for fuck's sake?

● ● ●

Today I took my antidepressant medication nine hours late.

Looked up suicide again on the Internet. Very interesting. Very harrowing. Oddly compelling.

Found out about all sorts of methods. Realized that someone is probably committing suicide right now. I ache for them, and a curious darkness bleeds into my brain. I can't think, can't focus. Feel lifeless, listless, hollow. I can't believe I actually survived last year. I came too close to dying…too often.

They would have done it by now. Are they in pain? Or gone? In a few hours someone will find them. I'll be asleep. I'll wake up, eat breakfast. While a family tears itself apart and drowns.

I'll tell you what I miss, now that I'm "better" (or getting there). I miss that almost orgasmic thrill that would zip through me when I flicked through cookbooks. I miss the slow savoring of imaginary texture and moisture and taste, the careful turning of pages, the solemn visual dissection of each picture. It doesn't feel the same anymore.

But I suppose I have to convince myself that that's a good thing. "I suppose" doesn't mean I will. There are many things I should do and very few I seriously consider.

Is there some magical, honeycombed paradise called "Recovery"? That I'll just stumble into one day while doing my crossword or cuddling the cat?

They're dead. I wonder if they regret it. After all, to feel better you sort of have to be *alive*.

To: You
From: Me

Is it so hard to understand? I'm falling in love with you.

Hurry up and slap me out of it. I'm supposed to be above this emotional drivel.

I'm having to abstain from eating my mango jelly and custard and listening to Jeff Buckley because it's only making it worse.

Don't worry...I'll get over it. Just take it as a compliment.

So I'm guessing it isn't commonplace to go around telling guys you love them. I'm not well practiced in the wiles of boyfriend-nabbing in its current context.

He didn't reply to my e-mail. It does hurt. It hurts behind my ribs. A bloated stomach from comfort/binge eating does nothing to boost my confidence, either. Whoops. I just remembered that he is actually *a boy*. Yes. There I was treating him as an emotionally cavernous human, when I realized that he's an eighteen-year-old boy. Of course. *You just don't go around saying things like that to eighteen-year-old boys*. Silly.

This perhaps calls for some man-hating, Germaine Greer-ness.

I just want to run away and become someone else...just vanish and start somewhere new. A new Lucy.

. . .

I'm sending that boy I can't stop thinking about another e-mail, now that a few days have passed and I feel sufficiently ashamed of my sudden honesty. I feel as though I ought to explain it.

To: You, again
From: Me, again

This time last year I was put on suicide watch. I'm having a tough time as the weather gets colder. Memories can be very strong. I'm not going to go into details, because I'm not even sure if I can ascertain the realities myself.

It's weird entering the same period of year that I almost died in last year. I would have been in hospital, but there was no bed free. Thank God. This time last year, I made the decision against starving myself to death. The fact I was killing my brain, my (somewhat latent, at that point) ambition, and the effect I was having on my mum ultimately decided it for me.

Then, well, the depression. The fucking black dog in all his terrifying glory. That's when my parents were told never to leave me by myself. When my school not-so-politely told me that I should drop out, forfeit being head prefect, and shut myself up in inpatient therapy. Yeah, right. I'm very perverse. If someone tells me I can't do something, I go and fucking do it.

I can't say this in person because...I start crying. And that's somewhat embarrassing and a bit of a mood dampener.

The combination of the antidepressants and tranquillizers disembodied my mind...I'd float above myself. Completely disconnected and numb. This lasted for months and months. Utter apathy. Except when it came to the possibility of starving myself into oblivion or finishing myself off. Then my mind was wonderfully animated.

That's why I have this sudden urge to do everything; to feel things and experience things, and see things and say things and watch people...

Mainly because I didn't realize how much I'd sacrificed until I started claiming emotion, laughter, friendships, and life back. The intense shock and seeping warmth of feeling things again is addictive.

In the future, it won't matter as much. But now, as I struggle with the fragile aftermath, it explains a lot about myself.

· · ·

The smell of autumn. The nipping chill to the air in the afternoon when I walk. Shivering in and out of the shower.

I keep having these awful flashbacks.

I walk for half an hour to my Grandma's nursing home where I watched her die. Walking past seems to take an age and a half, wading through memories and that familiar smell. That awful smell of warm food, elderly bodies, disinfectant, and mustiness.

I used to give her daffodils. In their little plastic vase, they'd smile and bob cheekily on her table. Filling the heavy room with their orange tang (gently undercut with the very scent of happiness). I'd hold them up to her nose, even though she couldn't smell, and let her pretend to forget the plastic floor, the commode, the incoherent babbling from the room down the hall. And while I held her hand (bruised, crinkled, childishly pink), I would notice the daffodils instead of the urine; the daffodils instead of the jerking veterans and the wheelchairs and the soiled nappies and the watery broccoli.

I looked in the front door, tried to see into that familiar corridor, remember anything and everything...but I couldn't. So I kept walking, sped up, stopped, hesitated, felt tears tingle in my nose and my throat constricting.

I just loved her so much.

· · ·

Tonight can be nicely summed up by:

Apathy
Apathy and shallow breath,
Blankness of mind
And eye.
Sit.
Stare.
Breathe?
Unfinished tails of thought,
Desires abridged into a kind of buzzing
Behind the temple.
Not there, but partly.
Perhaps. Vacant frustration,
An irritation of sorts
As the mind sleeps
And limbs stir thickly.
The cue is to breathe.
In
Out.
Impassive torture.

• • •

I just saw my psychiatrist. We're going to start looking at the core issue behind all of the anorexia and depression: that of personal inadequacy. I left feeling a little more optimistic.

Bought some vegetarian sushi and Engels' *Socialism: Utopian and Scientific* on my way home.

I am forgotten.

I can't evict him from my mind. I was too easy. Too eager. Guys don't like that apparently. They like a chase or at least a few games of hard-to-get. I just don't do that. I'm sick of games: I've been playing them all my life.

I don't feel entirely "here." Maybe it isn't depression. Maybe I'm genuinely insane. It's a possibility, of course. Still, it's all very interesting. Having the world flash and writhe before your eyes is highly…peculiar. Compelling, but exhaustingly so.

But I'm getting so much better. Aren't I? I've moved on from the numb automaton stage of recovery. I can feel.

Recovery. The past seems like a fabricated dream...I romanticize the horror, pine after the slow suicide, gloss over the shivering, the cold. The spaces and the skin and the bones. Bah! I'm moving on. I have to. I literally have one other option: death. Pure and simple. That's what anorexia is: a death wish.

There's too much I want to do and experience, right? I do want to live, don't I? Do I? I have said I feel too intensely for some people. I don't do things by halves. I fall in love—and I do so completely. No emotion seems to have a half-life with me. It's all *now*, deeply now and here; heart, mind, soul, eyes.

I want sex, drugs, riotous camping trips with friends, naked beach swims, sleepless nights in the city, conversations with everybody, hugs from strangers. I want to buy lunch for homeless people, drive into my soul and that of others, go to eardrum-bursting concerts, dance in the rain, ask difficult questions, knit myself and others into life and memory. What is so wrong with me? I confuse myself. I'm not sure what it is I want and whether I can get away with or succeed at any of it. Inadequacy of soul, of purpose, of self...

I just want to sleep. Watching the autumn leaves sun themselves, I'm reminded of the utter transparency of all of this. Of me, of life, of Earth...of everything. So why bother struggling on and giving meaning to that which has none?

Because it's all we have, I suppose.

To: You, once more
From: Me, yet again

Let's throw pink paint bombs at depression, forget about premature Jeff Buckley-induced assertions of love, and eat cupcakes.

Send. Sigh. Self-torture.

• • •

Again, again, again. Purging in the shower.

I'm not doing it every day, that's the main thing. It's my last-resort coping mechanism.

Ugh. Excuses. Shut up.

This is just carrying me over this rough patch. Once I start eating a little more regularly and am not so stressed out about university and that bloody boy, I won't need to do it because I'll be eating properly.

More excuses.

And, as I am aware every morning when I step on the scales, doing it just makes me put on even more weight. I do realize that I can't do this, on and off, indefinitely. I need to stop.

I…don't really like myself at the moment.

Come on Luce. *Come on.* I wonder if I ever will succeed in destroying myself. Maybe this is all a game…a waiting period. A false limbo. A make-believe life to while away the time between now and when I do actually go under.

Oh fuck that. That's a tad morbid for this time of night. Get over yourself, girl. Start focusing on things that will make you and those you love happy. Isn't that what it's all about? Happiness? And finding it?

But I'm getting a bit sick of that excuse for the meaning of life. So "happiness" is just sitting in a little pink box somewhere waiting to be found. Happy people irritate me, remember? It's fake and it's a dream, a construct. A fairy-tale to hide the black. Conveniently packaged up and waiting to be found by that lucky individual.

You cynic, Luce. I'm sure it was you who was happy yesterday, or the day before. Something like that.

Tomorrow will be better. Sitting around at home on public holidays isn't good for me.

• • •

Today I went for a walk and wanted to die.

That's all, really.

I'm not exaggerating. I have no energy for exaggeration when the numbness takes over.

It was dark and cool; I stayed away from the harsh streetlights. I just wanted to fade into shadow. To keep walking into the black indefinitely. I lingered in the dark, hoping someone would come along and try to kill me or attack me or make me feel something other than this dreadful gray.

I'm still here. It didn't work.

At home I ate and ate in some awful attempt to fill something bottomless. My body crumpled into bed. I slept between breakfast and lunch, saw a friend, slept between seeing her and now. I am…weak. Weak and half-heartedly skirting the black. I don't really think I can avoid it. Maybe I'm already there. It's possible. I'm not in touch with myself at the moment.

I will have to see the special consideration people at university. I have a massive assignment due in a couple of days. I am not better. I'm nowhere near better. I can't predict when I'll fall or how long I'll be under.

Breathing is too much effort.

● ● ●

I watched the autumn leaves burn against the sky. Burning in the gold of the last sunlight, against the gray clouds.

I walked down George Street and watched more people. Flicking from face to face, from mood to mood.

I went to my Law lecture about children in detention centers and once again felt disgusted to be Australian. Nothing new, of course. Sitting in the quad and leaning back against the cool sandstone, I ate a thick slice of squishy banana bread and drank a soy cappuccino.

I seem to be an international-students magnet. It was the same at school. A Korean girl came up to me and just started talking. And talking. We spent about half an hour talking. Well…not really talking. More gesturing and laughing at jokes we pretended to understand. She eventually told me that she wanted an Australian friend she could practice English with. So now she has my number. She was sweet, if a tad eager.

I lay on the lawn and fell asleep while reading *Le Morte d'Arthur* for English. Actually, I dozed out of sheer laziness: the clouds were too dazzling in the sun for me to keep squinting.

Then I sat in the library and tried my best to look scholarly whilst highlighting my history notes with a blue highlighter. It was very warm. The light was stormily graying outside. I hit my head on the desk. I'd fallen asleep.

While in the library, I managed to maintain a light and fluffy conversation with the exact type of boy I don't normally like, i.e. boy boys. Like *real* ones. With thickset heads and rugby backs. The ones you can just imagine sitting down to watch sport with a beer.

Oh, and I was happy for a while. But then tiredness ceded to absolute hyperactivity later in the evening.

As usual, Mum asked me if it was my medication playing up.

As usual, I said that yes, it was.

Actually, I think it was just me.

Me and my head full of gold leaves.

• • •

Today I threw up. Then I had the most enormous plate of Thai takeaway possible with a friend. It was really good.

Don't judge me. I'm dealing with it, okay?

• • •

Oh shit. That's why. Oh shit. **Oh shit.**

I threw up my medication this morning.

That explains a lot.

Why couldn't I just finish myself off properly the first time?

• • •

Oh ho. *I'm on to you, Luce.*

You can't fool me. No sirree.

You're just being a little drama queen. Want a little action in your life, that's it, hey?

Feeling a bit too…normal?

It's scary having normal looking thighs, isn't it? And arms that actually look like arms?

Okay. Here's the new plan.

Firstly, go back to –kilograms. That was a healthy weight, right? I can do that. I put on too much, too quickly. I just need to slow down.

Secondly, for God's sake stop starting the day off with a binge. *You know what that leads to. Yes. And then in the afternoon you repeat the process, because you were so worried about the morning.*

And besides, it's giving you mouth ulcers.

Next, stop picking at your face as a way of punishing yourself. You're ugly enough as it is. You certainly don't need to exacerbate the problem by adding an army of inflamed red bits. This includes your habit of attacking legs, arms, chest, and stomach. Lastly, find a way to deal, for God's sake. Preferably a way that involves catching up on all your university reading.

. . .

I'm not confident enough to wear the clothes I've bought. They're too...edgy for me. Too fashionable. They'll boycott my aim to fade into shop windows and melt into the asphalt.

Stripes and spots and color. Some days I just want an eraser.

. . .

When the cold weather creeps into my fingers, memories hang around me in some flat gray pall.

Why am I like this? What are other people like? I wouldn't know. I gravitate toward similarly dark minds. The black fades and billows depending on the time of day...depending on triggers...depending on little, inconsequential things...

I have an idea of who I am...but I can't be sure of the definitive lines between me, my medication, what I want others to see me as, and the remnants of who I used to try to be.

I know I'm shy, but only around people I like and whom I respect. I can also be headily confident...ridiculously confident. I know I'm rigidly reserved, but that's softening. I know I'm empathetic and compassionate and self-critical. I know I'm too polite for some people and too loud for others. I know I'm a perfectionist, that I'm disorganized, depressive, disposed to melancholy, romantic (not in the modern sense); and I know I'm scared of living, to a certain extent. But what am I, exactly? I love and hate food...I have a tendency to self-destruct; I exaggerate; I crave both attention and invisibility, company and solitude. I have an unsettling fascination with suicide.

Maybe it's all just a construct. Maybe in my attempt to re-find myself, I lost what I really was before. But why would I want to be like that again?

I can feel myself slipping back into my old habits. I need to keep writing to remind myself of myself, and to prevent myself from giving into the darker thoughts hovering just there.

You know what Lucy? You're a complete drain on everybody.

Shut up, please.

People pity you. They'll drop away soon enough. When the novelty wears off. Do you honestly think anyone worthwhile wants to hang around with someone as insecure and emotional as you?

I can't let myself believe that again.

You were at Darling Harbour yesterday. Walking over that bridge. Staring at the road and traffic below. Half-heartedly contemplating what would happen if you just…

Yes, but I didn't. I never seriously considered it. It was just a spur of the moment "I wonder what it would feel like if…"

Tears are prickling in my nose…but I still feel curiously shunted from myself.

Today was good, actually. It's just the night…and no human contact makes me pensive.

That's it. I feel…*raw*.

． ． ．

I've been teething on a particularly good panini roll. Crusty…squishy…holey…Mmm. I still have some flour on my nose from its futile defense.

I think I might pop up to the second-hand bookshop. I'm in need of some musty, dog-eared classics. And I am alone. I need distraction from myself.

． ． ．

Good God, I feel repulsive.

It is taking everything I have not to throw up.

I've taken my medication, dammit. So I actually cannot afford to throw it up. Unless I want to throw myself in the deep end again for another week. Another week of contemplating throwing myself off bridges.

Walking out of university today, the sight of red autumn leaves against a sulking deep gray sky and the little sandstone gatekeeper's cottage made me catch my breath. With the chill in the air, I could have been walking through Oxford. I kept the dream alive until I walked into a green sign telling me that Sydney City was down the road.

I watched a hunched old man drag himself up Parramatta Road. That got me thinking. On the bus I made unintelligible scribbles about everything I could think of in my history reader. Let me try to decipher some of them:

1. *Humanity as self-crippling. Yoke of overreaching advancement.*

2. *Pink shirted, balletic gesticulator. In a black sports car. His hand moving as though he were addressing the Business Council of Australia or something.*

3. *Capitalism inevitable considering the innate vices of humanity...*

4. *... As inherently selfish, self-serving, profit-seeking, inward-looking.*

5. *Where are the thinkers?*

6. *Intrinsic self-anxiety.*

7. *The idea of "nation" is intangible; a psychological state rather than a geographical reality.*

8. *Are we all essentially remote beings?*

9. *Jesus, how depressing. But why this assumed superiority that "allows" me to make judgments upon that which I am blindly and irrevocably bound to and a part of?*

Ha. What a load of shit. Me trying to feel intellectual on Sydney public transport.

• • •

My psychiatrist is insisting I see her soon. Insisting. I haven't seen her for a couple of weeks because I hate going there so much. The smell, the shape of the rooms—it's all so horribly familiar. It makes me sweat. I can't do this. It just brings back everything so forcefully. I'd prefer to leave it hidden and undisturbed.

I've just eaten and spat out three-quarters of my Easter chocolate. I vomited up the ones I actually ate. Chocolate is not fun to purge. And I am ashamed.

I feel like a failure. An imposter. I don't think I can really do anything. I don't want to be able to just DO things; I want to do things EXCEPTIONALLY. There's too much I don't know and, what's more, *cannot* know while I'm in this state.

But when I put on weight, I panic. It's symbolic of everything I don't want to be. I am slim and healthy. That should thrill me. Instead, it terrifies me. It's too normal. It doesn't feel safe.

It's easier at university because no one knows or suspects anything. With my older friends, there's a role to play: that of recovering-anorexic-who-is-by-association-scared-of-food-and-self-obsessed.

I think it isn't love that I'm looking for. It's more of a total desire for unconditional companionship.

I wish my imagination would tone down a shade or two. To sepia, instead of its current 256-bit color scheme.

Did I mention I've been purging a lot lately? Now I have a pain in my chest and pink spots in my eyes. Maybe I'll die and save myself all the trouble of living, chocolate eggs, and unrequited adoration.

• • •

I hid in the library toilets for a while at university, but instead of looking at the toilet seat, I was accosted by my thighs. I know I'm being silly, but they actually were obese. Utterly disgusting. I looked at them and poked at them in utter, total, complete disgust and disbelief.

I came home and painted my fingernails red.

I'm low. I don't cry, but tears keep burning behind my eyes.

All the red leaves have gone from the tree outside my window. I opened my curtains this morning expecting to see them flaming in the morning sun, as usual, but they were gone. The rain butchered them. They're lying limp and brown on the lawn.

• • •

I spend hours, literally hours, in bookshops. Just cruising the shelves, reading, picking out little gems.

There was this woman on the bus today, and she just wouldn't stop picking her nose. I looked at her and she looked right back at me, finger stuffed up her nostril, gyrating wildly. And then, five minutes later, she did it again. That must have been one serious booger she had going there.

There are lots of yummy boys around. And since I've been wearing my hair down and low-cut, polka-dotted dresses, I've been getting a few looks...

And guess what? *I even talk to some of them.* (Giggle.)

Ooooh, Lucy. And sometimes I get so sexually frustrated I just want to drag them behind a building and have them. *Like that.*

• • •

I have never felt so utterly devoid of purpose.

Defunct. Vacant.

My face has slackened into a shocked neutral that is too hard to change: one eyebrow partly raised, eyes wide, pupils dilated, uneven jaw, and half a frown.

I've been standing in the bathroom looking at my face and the spots on my dress for twenty minutes. My arms were crossed. They were too tired to hang by my sides on their own.

I cannot blink. I'm breathing fluid air voluntarily. When my mind slides into brief moments of total apathy, I forget to breathe altogether.

My head was too heavy. So I leant my forehead against the bathroom wall. Against the cool tiles.

Breathe. Once every ten seconds if I'm lucky.

Deadened. I can hardly move my fingers. Indescribable. I haven't the energy. And all the while...a complete absence of value. I am transparent; I dissolve and swallow silence.

Gone. I'm somewhere outside of myself. I think I might be going mad.

• • •

I slept for most of the morning. To avoid having to face the day.

I've been thinking about my grandma. I've been thinking about that night when Mum and I stood by her bed in that nursing home, listening to her breathing. Her faint hiccups, the rattling of a deep breath. Her face was expressionless, motionless; the face I had loved for years and years was half buried in those crisp white pillows of institution. Her hands were warm, for once.

Every time a space of seconds would pass without her breathing, I would stand absolutely still, waiting—wishing—for the next one, but with a heavy heart almost hoping not. I would look at her daffodils, as twenty seconds—thirty—passed, before a faint breath would allay the drumming of my heart (in my mouth, it felt).

But then, a minute. More. I barely breathed. Not taking my eyes off her face, I tried to remember if I'd opened the window. It suddenly seemed desperately necessary that the window be open.

"Is the window open?" I remember asking, below even a whisper. I felt Mum nod.

I watched that dear face as it mottled yellow and mauve. I leant over and took her hand.

It was cold. I bent down and kissed her on the forehead, my eyes closed to the brown mucus on her pillow or that horrible, horrible color of skin.

Tight-lipped, Mum was crying. Noiselessly, brokenly.

I can't remember what happened to the daffodils.

• • •

It was cold today. I sat in the library for three hours, skipping lectures I just couldn't bring myself to go to, nodding in the warmth, sunning my fingers and doing a monster crossword.

I had an appointment with the student disability services, on the warm, hushed seventh level of the education building. I sat next to a lanky boy called Troy. A girl hurried in and asked for an urgent consultation. I wondered why they were here. What their "problems" were. Thankful they didn't know mine was anorexia—they'd have no reason to judge my current weight. *Well, she certainly doesn't look anorexic.*

I was ushered into a poky little blue room. It was quite nice inside: bright, clean, friendly. A big poster on the wall said "Don't DIS my ABILITY." There was a potted plant, I think. Deidre (I could be wrong here), with curly moppish hair and motherly curves, bounced into the room. I spoke robotically, told her I was in recovery from anorexia and depression. Told her of the effects. Held back tears, defiantly. Tried to discreetly make my collarbones poke out a little bit, so she wouldn't think I was lying.

Whether that worked or not, she must have realized I wasn't lying.

So now I have exam provisions. And a counseling service at my disposal.

The cold is different to what it was last year. It doesn't linger in my bones anymore. It tightens and numbs my skin pleasantly, but that is all. I walked home in the crisp gray light of 5 p.m., moving with the sharp wind. Gray storm clouds washed with a sickly pink. Spitting rain. Lonely streets.

It was lovely.

But now I'm down again. I know what it is. I have two weeks left of first semester, and I'm at the end of my tether. It's been a long term. A long, new, foreign, exciting, scary, confronting term.

• • •

I'm mentally static tonight. Slack. Relaxed. Too fluid. Psychologically flabby.

- *Today I ate too much.*

- *Today I gave a presentation in English.*

- *Today I didn't skip any lectures.*

- *Today I accidentally spent money on a PJ Harvey CD and another Jeff Buckley CD to add to my burgeoning collection.*

- *Today I wore my new boots; smelt my new boots; tried to ignore my sore feet from wearing my new boots all day.*

- *Today I felt squished, flat, deadpan, and lifeless.*

- *Today I put away the piles and piles of clothes I've been stacking around my room for the past three months.*

- *Today I lined my shoes up in a nice, colorful line.*

- *Today I cooked corn and carrot fritters.*

- *Today I had two Le Petit Ecolier biscuits against my will, but freely chosen. Yes, that does make sense.*

And now:

- *I am going to have a shower.*
- *I am going to get into bed.*
- *I am going to rip out all the monster crosswords from my old-fogey magazines.*
- *I'm going to highlight my Law notes with a pink highlighter.*
- *I am going to do some sit-ups.*
- *I am going to see whether that boy has logged into MySpace today. I will then obsess until I slip into sleepy-land.*

That's all I can deal with at the present time.

• • •

Today in my Law seminar I decided that I would change the world.

Then, I tripped into a little drab slump. I hid in the toilets. I strung out any energy I had, trying to be sociable and not too withdrawn. In my self-frustration, I told one of my closest Law friends about the anorexia and depression and recovery. I was effectively apologizing and making an excuse for my limpness.

I'm glad I told her. I have been meaning to for a while.

• • •

This is a new phenomenon. I'm still having to pinch myself. I can feel; it's okay to feel. I can express how I feel. It isn't a weakness.

I want to write a book. I want to write a book primarily concerned with anorexia, depression, and recovery. And I want to show people the joy of little tiny things, the joys that you have to hunt down for survival. I used to scoff at these. When Mum showed me a tree on fire in the sun, I used to laugh at her.

"So what? It's a tree."

I still laugh at her. But it's different. I laugh because I find it difficult to share those moments of utter beauty with anyone. If I'm to experience them…drown in them…I need to do so alone.

I'm a hopeless case. I did have a very low slump today. I think I may have briefly mentioned it; or maybe not. My imaginings bleed into my reality frequently.

I felt utterly base. Low. Hollow. Nothing. Unworthy of attention. A fraud. A boring fraud. I wanted to barrel down into the earth or hide in my wardrobe. As it was, at university, I was an hour away from home. An hour of *public transport* away from home. I actually didn't think I could do it.

So I went and hid in the toilets. Then I hid behind a corner and called Mum. I forced myself to go to the top level of Manning Bar to sit with some friends. I sat there and listened to their chatter…and felt cut off, lonely, exiled. My plaster mask rapidly deteriorated. The smile slid into a grotesque grimace.

• • •

She's very self-conscious. She watches her thighs get bigger; pokes at the flabby bits. Presses them down into the sofa to make them spread. Looks at them, eyes squinting.

"*Fat*," she says.

But she also knows that she isn't. She really can't be. She has to be logical, she says. She's underweight and therefore can't possibly be fat. But others don't understand that all weight is relative, that she not only doesn't want to be fat, she doesn't want to be merely thin either. She wants to be emaciated. Then she laughs at herself for being so ridiculous. And then she sighs because she doesn't feel ridiculous…because it all seems painfully necessary.

She argues. She needs a good shout to help relieve some of the frustration. Frustration at not being able to dedicate herself in entirety to anorexia, frustration in her inability to let go and *live*.

She's sitting before the computer now…jiggling legs…picking at her mouth…trying to work out what to say. She sits up straight automatically as this burns more calories. Then she thinks about university this year. Thinks about the marshmallows she just ate. Clenches her teeth and hisses to herself:

"*I will do this.*"

• • •

I wore my polka dots again today with black tights, black shoes, and my little cropped red cardigan.

I came home and binged. A jar of nuts, cereal, bread. I haven't vomited in two weeks, but I couldn't bring myself to leave all that food sitting like rock in my stomach today. I panicked and brought it all back up. I have told Mum about the vomiting in the past. Sometimes I can't keep it from her. But if she knew how often...

I *am* getting better. It's the depression that drags me under backwards. It's the depression that's so hard to lift. It's hard to breathe when your head is being squeezed and slapped around. Or when your mind melts into complete apathy and nonfeeling.

Still, I'm learning.

• • •

I will not purge.

I will not purge.

I will not purge.

That's the easy option. I've never gone for the easy option.

I will not do it.

No.

It hurts, yes. I feel very uncomfortable. My thighs are spreading and that food is sitting like a lump of lead in my stomach.

But I won't do it. I did it yesterday. And all last week.

It's okay. It's okay. You're finding yourself. You are not defined by how well you can self-destruct or how frail you can make yourself. That is no personality. That's a cover-up.

Write. Something. Anything. Just don't do it.

Okay.

• • •

I cried. I cried in squeaks and gasps. As though I was trying to expel something from my body.

I got up from my bed after a while. Stood and looked at myself in the mirror. Swollen eyes, dilated pupils. A slack mouth. I looked and looked until my peripheral vision faded and all I could see was that familiar reflection in the mirror. It was me and my body; my head strangely disconnected from that form in the mirror. She didn't move. I didn't move. We just looked at each other blankly, but not without sympathy. I had lost myself in the mirror, in a portrait of myself.

I don't know how I got out. Perhaps it was my dog barking that wrenched me back into reality. I took my clothes off slowly. Folded them neatly.

Then I backed off a little. Looked at my whole body in the mirror. I tensed my thighs. *Still thin.* Brought my arms up into an arabesque, second, first, fifth. Still thin. I stretched and curled and my ribs danced beneath my skin. If I stood…like this…I could almost pretend I was five kilograms lighter. Or more.

Perhaps I am still thin. Perhaps. I have been exercising a lot more. Walking everywhere, multiple hours a day. My thighs are toned. Muscle? It weighs more than fat, right? Because I fancied for one fleeting second that I looked acceptable. Certainly not *thin*, but on the thin side of slim.

That's good, isn't it? My body is being very stubborn. It is refusing to move. It doesn't go up and it doesn't go down. It's hanging on to this new weight for all it's worth. Is that a sign? It's always been easy for me to go up…easy for me to go down. Now I just can't. It's comforting, in a way.

Today may be better. It feels better. I have another extension on my assignment until Wednesday. It's okay, you know?

It is, I think. We'll see. We'll see.

• • •

I made a new friend today. She's very colorful. Fiercely intelligent. She writes *beautifully*.

I feel very inferior, actually.

But that's nothing new.

• • •

I found a lovely recipe for ricotta hotcakes with orange curd.

One day…soon-ish…I'll have my own wee apartment. Or studio. It must be small. There will be a little cat called Dot. Bookcases lining one of the walls to the ceiling. My drawings on the walls. A cozy, shiny kitchen with a cupboard full of organic cereals. Potted plants. Tall windows. Blue, cream, beige. Yellow.

And I'll get up in the morning and make ricotta hotcakes with orange curd.

Then I'll water those potted plants and read the paper in the sun. Write. Go for a walk. Plan my imminent saving-of-the-world. Perhaps do some work. Wear my stripy multi-colored socks. Sing along to my music.

Tomorrow I will wear my red stockings.

• • •

My evening: cappuccinos, marshmallows in cappuccinos, desperate legal-research-assignment-poking, tomato pasta, dried fruit, PJ Harvey, and wooden beads.

I talked for an hour to a homeless man in the city. I see him in the same spot every week, and as I walked past, he said I had a lovely smile. I kept walking…but then turned back. Stood there in thirteen degrees (i.e., exceptionally cold for Sydney) and listened to a history of his privations over the past decade. He has a commerce degree. He was helping support a twenty-four-year-old with two babies (he was…sixty-five?). He was spat on last week. He needs to get to Sweden…and he has a sneaking suspicion that the twenty-four-year-old is actually in love with him. Ahem. I eventually excused myself, told him that as soon as I got paid, I'd be helping in any way that I could, and wished him the absolute best of luck with everything.

I wonder what homeless people do at night. You know, in winter. It makes me…heavily sad.

I got off the bus in Mosman and started walking home in the dark and in the streetlights. I recognized one of the guys from my legal research class. He had a blonde girl hanging off him. I laughed shrilly and accepted his offer to drive me home. Regaled them both with stories about my day. Had them laughing. Had myself laughing. Carried myself off wonderfully, I think. Not a care in the world.

Home. Bedroom.

I don't have much luck, do I? I'm not terrifically successful in the relationship department. I'm apparently a great friend. Full stop. No one has ever fallen in love with me. I read people wrongly so that I'm constantly hit in the face when I realize that they meant nothing all along. I mean…there must be something intrinsically wrong with me. Everyone else seems to cope well enough. What is it about me?

● ● ●

I didn't think I could get home today. Some may know that feeling when everything just falls flat. When the disguise, the energy, the drive to do *anything* just…cowers…and you're left standing, by your-self, psychologically naked and utterly, utterly vulnerable.

I got home, eventually. After spending more money on cute little cardigans.

I'm now coming down from a manic high. I ate a (normal) dinner. I purged (some of) it. I then binged spectacularly because I felt so goddamn awful. And this time I let it be my punishment: I didn't purge. So I danced around crazily for about half an hour. Cut out my recipes. Decided (stupidly) that I should look at some old photos of me from last year.

Dumb. Dumb, dumb, dumb.

Just for good measure, I went through my school diary as well. Fingered the weeks and weeks and months and months' worth of pages that I must have fingered this time last year, when I was –kilo-grams lighter.

I took one last look at a photo showing that harrowed face and pale, pale skin and slid the photo back into its little yellow envelope. Then I realized that what I had put in the envelope was me and not me, at the same time.

I'm…drained. Just drained. Drained and…knobbly. In a fatty sense. Not a bony sense. But don't talk sense to me…*you of all people know how irrational this is.*

● ● ●

I'm wrapped up in my blue mohair blanket, eating Vegemite with a spoon from the jar and listening to the rain sing outside.

And intermittently cutting out recipes from magazines.

What to say? Not much. I have one major Law assignment due this week. It's a frustratingly enormous topic—the role of interna-tional law in domestic policy.

It's been gloriously chilly today. I stepped out in the purpled gray light of 5 p.m., into nine degrees, to walk the dog to the postbox. The rain was resting in slick mirrors on the new black asphalt, the clouds were hanging low and dark, and there was no one anywhere. The silence cuddled the little red lane.

It was beautiful. I click-clacked my way to the postbox in my new boots and came back with hands unfeeling from the cold, cheeks red and round, and my hair all over the place.

If I don't think about things too deeply, I can deal with them.

I'm okay. I am –kilograms at the moment. I'm comforted by knowing that that's where my muse is at. My "muse" and I met over the same "pro-ana" forum, at about the same time as I met A.

I am myself. I am self-sufficient. I am worth the attention of others. I don't have to be loved by everyone. I don't have to be the best at everything. I just have to be true to myself.

Still, it's a hard pill to swallow. That idea that I don't have to be the best, and what's more, that I can't be the best at the moment. I'm still teaching myself how to live, remember?

I'm still getting used to the idea of me as distinct from other people. I don't need to cut myself up into cute little shapes that laugh and smile all the time.

So I read Kafka while walking down George Street. So I do crosswords in public. So I actually like reading and like intellectual discussions and appreciate art and music and poetry.

Stuff the world and its little paper cutouts. They're boring.

• • •

Today I made banana spice muffins.

They're very squishy and moist and bouncy. With a thin, crispy top.

I hate the word "moist." I was desperately trying to think of any other word that would describe the texture…but "wet" just didn't cut it. For all of English's fortes, it seriously neglects the describing-of-food section. Damp? Nah. Negative moldy connotations or implied sogginess.

Alas…it had to be moist.

Let me just consult my dear friend Mr. Thesaurus.

"**moist** *adj* – wet."

Helpful.

I've eaten a lot. I refuse to compensate. I will sit here and think of the wonders it will do for my brain while I sleep tonight. (And besides, I danced crazily to the Beatles for about half an hour.)

My mood is dropping. I'm going to have to counter this quickly with sleep. Otherwise, I'll be awake all night worrying about people.

I need to brush my teeth. Convince myself that I'm loved. Jump into bed. Pull the covers up to my nose. Shed some theatrical tears. Listen to silly music and bop my hips around on the mattress.

I wish I knew where I was going.

. . .

Today I got as far as the Town Hall in the middle of the city. I watched the clouds split behind that sandstone steeple and the sun erupt through an opaque fog.

Then I turned on my heel and walked. It was too big. The world was too big and there were too many people. And at the same time I was too big, too noticeable. *Please, God, let me melt into the pavement.*

I walked to Hyde Park. Felt on show, spotlighted, searingly obvious. I needed to speak to someone, see someone who understood, but A was at work.

So I came home. That was hard in itself. I hate it when I suddenly find myself in the city, a moment past contentedness, when you realize that you *just have to get out*, just have to hide, leave, recoil...yet you still have to walk down the busiest streets in the city, manage a bus full of people, *and* walk home when all the schools are being let out.

People, people, people.

Preeeeesenting as a foil to all the colorful crazy women of the world: GRAYSCALE LUCY! She'll bore you to tears!

I have to stop that. *Stop that.*

I wish I had piles and piles of money, so I could go out and buy a heap of crazy things. To color me in, so to speak. *Ahh, but that would make no difference. You'd still be YOU.*

This is hard and lonely.

I was –kilograms this morning. I sighed with relief. How could that be? Lose weight *and* eat an entire block of Lindt chocolate the day before? I should start making this a habit. Eat a block of chocolate at 3 p.m., feel utterly ill, don't eat again until eight the next morning.

Sounds like a plan.

It's raining again. Singing in the drainpipe. Mum just came in. The grilling begins.

"How's it going, gorgeous?"

"Yeah."

"You sound better."

Oh. Goody. Just what I needed to hear.

It's coming down heavily now. In whistling shafts. The light feels sick. It's sticky...and yellow.

• • •

I have a head full of gold leaves again. They were beautiful. I stopped and stared. They were on fire against the gray sky.

Excuse me while I crash and burn with Sylvia Plath, contemplate life as a hermit in the Black Forest, and think about suicide as a psychological ploy. I feel like roasting marshmallows over my bedside lamp, but a) I have no marshmallows, and b) I have no bedside lamp.

• • •

My brain is sticky-taped together with chemicals. I forget how dependent I am on them until I forget to take them. Today has been a tad rickety. I couldn't make it into university. I sat at Circular Quay...and just couldn't get on that damn bus. I tried—God knows I tried—but my legs were as operative as lead. So I came home. Napped. Contemplated my sticky-taped self.

I'm skidding on self-doubt at the moment...I'm not quite sure who I am and why I should keep trying to find out. There was a girl on the bus when I was coming home with crazy blonde hair and carrying a crazy painting of some description. I just felt so insipid in comparison.

Hey. It takes time to put a self-esteem together. It's coming. Aiming for completion by the end of this year. Providing I have enough purple paint and sparkly stickers to decorate it.

• • •

Grocery shopping, oh wondrous grocery shopping. Lindt Ecuadorian chocolate, asparagus, panini, blue vein cheese, muesli with ginger-roasted oats and cashews...what else? Mango nectar, spicy tea biscuits, licorice, apples and plums...yum scrum.

And a wonderfully trashy *Cosmo* magazine. I stopped buying them a few years ago, but I need a laugh today. Which I'll get with the following stories: "What sex feels like for him," "My boobs went moldy," "Your break-up fantasies decoded," "What women look like down south." *Weird. I would have thought that was fairly well established…*

Oh ha. Ha, ha. Ahem. My gum tastes like Earl Grey tea with no sugar and a dash of milk…is that bizarre? It is supposed to be peppermint flavored.

* * *

I am low.

Guess what? This is life. I'm not perfect. Nowhere near it. I spend too much time convincing other people that I'm okay with a skip or a laugh or a stupid smile. No one could go through what happened to me the past two years and come out smooth. I'm damaged. There's a part of me that is still very bruised.

It's a slow process, this recovery. Tiny things keep me going. My friends. Lying in the sun at Sydney Uni. My coffee. Writing. Music.

I constantly feel the need to excuse myself, to explain to people why I'm the way I am…I have a very fragile confidence. I constantly feel inferior, inadequate, only just tolerated. I've never been good enough for myself and for my expectations. Gah…perfectionism. Innately compelled to be and do and have everything perfect and "better" than everyone else.

I can't make sense of my thoughts tonight.

Untangling them is futile.

Depression is ugly.

Oh but fuck…I can hardly believe how much better it is now than how it used to be. I still find it difficult to believe how bad it got—that couldn't have been me? How on earth did I exist like that for so long? Holding my breath in that black for so long.

I shouldn't even be here. But I am. Whoopdeefuckingdoo.

I refuse to give in to my state of mind at the moment. It's painful to challenge the thinking, but I will not let it convince me again that I'm an utter failure. Shit girl, you got through last year. That's amazing. You're studying Law at Sydney Uni. How the fuck did that happen? By chance? No. You can do it, damn it.

Stop feeling sorry for yourself. Stop undervaluing yourself. Get on track, for God's sake. You can't help others if you're killing yourself. If you were a failure, you would have given in long before this.

Stuff it, I say. Stuff it all. Play them all. It's all meaningless anyway. Stop giving in meekly and hatch some goddamn confidence, woman!

• • •

It has come to my attention that there are an awful lot of intellectual snobs studying Law who need a good kick up the bum. Or a squirt in the face. Law students are either affected with intellectual snobbery or intellectual denial. One is good for laughing at; the other is good for drinking with.

So. In the immortal words of a certain boy who I DO NOT remember (note emphasis): "So…do you like…stuff?" Now I just wish I'd said no, as stroking male egos is *rather* dangerous. They get a tad cocky and start talking about bugs. Well, this one did. And in his case, never stopped.

• • •

Why work when you can lounge around in the sun? In your new red angora cardigan? And think about little garden studios in London?

Ha, ha, ha. I am so behind at university, it really would be laughable if it was someone else.

• • •

Note to self: Starting university assessments at 9:30 p.m. the night before they are due does not work. It may have worked for school, but now it has been proven to fail spectacularly. I've never written such a woolly, indistinct, and wishy-washy essay as this one. I get confused just proofreading it. It's one long brain dribble. I mean, look at my ending sentence:

"One cannot veil reality in a vain attempt to mollify ego and deem it truth."

Good God. That's actually appalling.

• • •

Today I slept until 1:30 p.m. as I was too scared to go outside because the sky was too big.

I also

...froze

...dressed up

...had a good cry

...played with pastry

...hugged my UGG boots

...read with blue socks on

...wore my gray polka-dotted dress again

...ate blue cheese with marinated artichokes and asparagus

...pushed myself out of the house to walk the dog when it was dark and the sky was asleep

That is all. I didn't go to university. I couldn't go to university because of the sky, remember?

• • •

My psychiatrist told me about a girl in the hospital who had a BMI of.... They had managed to get her up to...and she was absolutely distraught as she thought herself so fat. I wonder how far I could have gone. Would I have been able to walk along the beach without even leaving a footprint? There's no point dwelling on it. And that idea's just stupid anyway.

I have to realize that the anorexia destroyed my life. It was terrifying. Not being able to control yourself is terrifying. The odd thing is, anorectics assume that they are in total control of this process, when in reality they are slowly and progressively handing control to the anorexia. To that demon. I never understood this and scoffed at my mum when she tried to make me listen to the logic. Anorexia has its own logic that isn't compatible with conventional reason. But I realize that now.

Maybe it wasn't so much about control as it was about wanting to be led? Maybe I was tired of leading and scared of being the one in control and wanted to forfeit that for subservience to a psychological disease? I'll never know. I can only speculate. We can only ever speculate.

• • •

I'm in a bit of a hole at the moment. I've put on weight and I can't stand it. I'm trying not to panic. Oh fuck. Here I go. I think about it, and it's like a hand clamping on my heart.

Stupid. All so stupid. I can't see outside myself except to worry about other people excessively. Other than that I'm stuck investigating my brain's bumfluff. In the dark.

• • •

Today I traipsed through an Asian Supermarket with A.

I was très intrigued by the green tea marshmallows. They were actually green.

The peanut crisps had black things in them, which was slightly concerning.

There was seaweed-everything everywhere. I like seaweed. Just not in the water.

Real crystallized ginger, green tea chocolate, pastries with bits coming out of them (it looked like toilet paper, but I'm assuming it wasn't), sweet potato and soy sauce chips, dried love prunes, as distinct from dried love plums.

It was faintly crazy. So now I'm organizing a grand Asian food fest.

• • •

He is very dear to me. I am very dear to him. But that is all.

And after seeing him today, I think I'm okay with that.

He traveled for half an hour through the rain and at a disruption to his packing for Europe to see me. I skipped an entire day of university to see him.

We sat and talked. He was tired and scruffled…we hugged. He kissed my forehead, I think. I can't remember.

It was getting dark. And colder. We walked down Pitt Street, me suffocating under that very familiar cloud of blackness.

We said goodbye on the corner, in the rain. Hugged for a very long time. Just held each other. I tried not to cry. I kissed him on the cheek. He turned, and walked away. I stood there in the rain. Hugging my unfurled umbrella to my chest. Rain running down my cheeks in the place of tears.

The air was throbbing on the bus. The sandstone wall: swinging past and staring. It is dark; I am dark. I have drowned myself. Left some part of me in the dark gutter of the city.

I stumble home in a funnel of black. Screaming lights: red, yellow, brilliant white. I trip into the darkness homewards, the trees and houses swaying on either side, my stockings wet from the rain, my face scrunched. I indulge in tears, hiding my wobbling head in the plastic of my umbrella. There is nobody watching. I feel ashamed and emotionally naked anyway.

I grip the handle of my umbrella tightly and feel my heart beat through my fingers. There is a car coming toward me, and it isn't going to stop. It would be so easy. The puddle; the road; the car; silence among the headlights.

I don't.

Somehow I slip home. Crouch in the darkness of my room. Shudder and shake.

Curled on my bed, a hand over my face, knees hugged under my chin. Eyes plastered open.

I dissect myself in a confusing tumble over the phone to K; crying and whispering and trying not to apologize for myself. I sob into Mum's hair. I stretch and claw my way out of myself and into the shower. Hot. Very hot. Tingling; goose bumps and steam. I must have stood there under the running water for about fifteen minutes before realizing I had to actually wash myself at some point. Slowly, carefully; not wanting to identify this body as mine.

• • •

The obsession with bones is very odd. It seems to get worse and worse with recovery, which is even more peculiar. What is it about? This adulation of frame? Of jutting edges and scarcely disguised clefts? Perhaps it's about wanting to strip everything back to the beginning, the very essence of being. Perhaps this reflects my need for order and simplicity in a chaotic and pressured life. As though I need to peel off all the unnecessary slabs and residue and expose myself for who I really am. For me. No longer hidden by fat and detritus. Odd. Now I have some of my rationality back, I spend a lot of time trying to reason why these processes and ideas hold such sway. I used to just accept them, because to think any other way would make me squirm and cry with terror.

· · ·

I could never truly express why I developed anorexia until I read this in *Wasted*. It clicked...and I felt the truth in a head rush.

> *The idea of my future simultaneously thrilled and terrified me, like standing at the lip of a very sheer cliff—I could fly, or fall. I didn't know how to fly, and I didn't want to fall. So I backed away from the cliff...*

...and ensconced myself in an insecurity-driven, expectations-ridden disorder. To punish myself, almost, for dreaming too much, for aspiring to too high a level. I wanted to ground myself completely, so I wouldn't have the chance to fly—and therefore, wouldn't have the chance to fail.

· · ·

I'm not sure I can articulate this, but I'll try.

I binged on pistachio nuts, of all things. Ate way beyond the point of satisfaction.

My head started spinning from panic. I felt physically ill. Mum came home from work at that moment, so I was trapped. I couldn't get it out of me. I had to do something to myself...I had to hurt myself, scratch myself, hit myself, something to express something that was grinding and cackling inside.

I stood outside the bathroom for fifteen minutes, my nails digging into my neck. I stood there in the half-light, unsure. I stumbled in towards the toilet and fell out again. I knew I had to take the dog for a walk. It was getting darker, and I didn't think I could go outside. I didn't want anyone seeing me. It was terrifying.

Something rose inside me. The anorexia, I suppose. It didn't speak, just created these intense conceptual feelings. The first was that I was a fucking, good-for-nothing loser and coward. The second was that I had failed. I can't even describe how vivid these feelings were. The words are sterile.

I stood in the hall and gripped my skull. I squeezed until my hands were white; I clenched my teeth until I thought they would shatter. I hit and hit and hit my thighs with my fists. I growled, I think. Gutturally. I had to get something out. I had to hurt myself.

Mum came with me while I walked the dog. I could feel my thighs jiggling slightly. Anger and absolute desperation. I gripped the leash and rubbed away at my neck until it was red and sore. I cried, but tried not to. Under cover of darkness.

Perhaps I am insane. I came in and threw myself at my bed, gripped my aching head, and lay there in a contorted, fetal curl. My eyes stared unseeingly at the ceiling, one arm splayed across my neck, unmoving, until it went numb. And now I'm typing this standing. I don't dare sit down and feel my thighs against the smooth white wood of the chair. I want to beat myself up. My neck is aching and I feel utterly ill. I want to throw myself off a cliff, a really rocky one.

Why?

I didn't purge.

• • •

What am I afraid of?

1. *Not doing well in philosophy.*

2. *Not doing well in history.*

3. *Not doing well in English.*

4. *Of people not liking me.*

5. *Of people being bored with me.*

6. *Putting on weight.*

7. *Eating.*

8. *Food.*

9. *Being rejected.*

10. *Of him not liking me.*

11. *Of him only liking me.*

12. *Of my gums receding.*

13. *Making a fool of myself.*

14. *Having people laugh at me.*

15. *Disappointing my mum.*

16. *Self-imploding for a second time.*

17. *Not self-imploding for a second time.*

18. *Actually having deep relationships with people.*

19. *Sex and intimacy.*

20. *Being disabled by shyness.*

21. *Not doing well enough in Law.*

22. *Of being alone.*

23. *Of getting dumb (what the hell is all this medication doing to my brain???).*

24. *Thinking too much of myself (so I just beat myself down).*

25. *Not getting all my study done before my exams start next Wednesday.*

26. *Being left out or ignored.*

27. *My stomach and thighs.*

28. *You getting tired of me.*

29. *Coming across as fake.*

30. *Caring too much.*

31. *Everything from tomorrow.*

• • •

It's raining—which I love—but it's not the weather that's particularly conducive to a positive change in mood. It's almost the end of semester and my exams are creeping up...my marks are falling and I've got one foot stuck in the depression. It has been a little difficult lately. But I've been writing and drawing...trying to convince myself that I don't need to change any part of me for anyone else. That I am my own person and should revel in that...

Ahh, I don't know.

• • •

A beautiful boy just gave me his number while I was at work.

Tall. Business suit. A lovely toothy smile. He was going around to all the shops for a bank or something. About an hour after he left, he came back in and said something incoherent along the lines of "I'll just leave my number with you...in case...someone...something, something."

So what, he'd be about twenty-six? Why would you come back into a women's clothing store two hours after you'd been through the area for your company and give the salesgirl your mobile number? Why not leave your business number?

Eeek. Oh yippee. Eekity. Oh dear. Let me try to excuse this. I don't get picked up. This is *me* we're talking about here.

Why would he do that? Why would he leave his mobile number with me? Is this some weird business code that I'm just misreading? Or is he trying to pick me up, here?

• • •

I am feeling good.

Perhaps...I am starting to find myself again. I can't be sure. I don't want to make too firm a judgment, just in case I am wrong.

• • •

Oh, I get so nervous. I'm seeing the boy who gave me his mobile number in a couple of days. It's just...he's a boy. I'm a silly shy little girl...four years younger than him, as it turns out.

I don't want to have to pretend anything, but I'm scared he won't like the real me. Or indeed, if I can even expose the "real me." It will be an exhausting act the first time.

But then again, I need to realize that sometimes people just don't "click." And that's through no fault of their own. It's just the way it is.

We're having coffee. I know I'll get overwhelmed when I first see him, simply because he doesn't look like a "boy," per se. I never noticed I had grown up. I never noticed that everybody else has been growing up. This boy is an absolutely gorgeous man—as much as typing that makes me cringe!

Mmmm. I have made one decision and that is not to pretend anything. If he doesn't like the fact that I sit on buses just to watch people, or that I love literature and solitude and arty-farty-ness, fine. I don't think he will, actually. He looks too "straight." I always need semi-gay boys. They're the only ones who understand me and the only ones I'm ever attracted to. Alpha-males and I don't fuse very often. I find them too amusing and too…male.

My stomach is twisting.

Note to self: When meeting this certain boy-man, I will NOT compromise my new self in an effort to be liked. I will just…be…*me*.

Full stop.

• • •

Sometimes I wonder what it is I have to offer the world. What it is I have to offer anyone. I have constructed myself for so long, I guess it's only natural I flounder in self-doubt as I strip back the artificial layers. I mean, *what if there's actually nothing underneath*? I could just keep peeling back indefinitely…only to discover that I diffused into the artificiality long ago.

Or maybe I can knit myself together? I think I can. I have been doing so for the past couple of months. I think I might even start liking "me." This new, raw, colorful, unmolded *me*.

I have issues; but they don't define me. I refuse to let them define me.

My calves are thin this morning. Or it could be the black tights. Last night Mum gestured toward the space around my waist and accused me of losing weight. But she's wrong. Instead, I'm putting it on.

I don't know. It's hard. I give myself no option. I'm letting myself live for the next decade until I'm twenty-eight…and then, if I'm in the same fragile headspace, I may consider going back to the anorexia and letting it take me. But I want to live first.

I won't really go back, I know that. But I like the fact that I *can*, if I want to.

· · ·

I feel very…tensely strung. I'm in a continuous state of holding-my-breath. Until I suddenly remember with a wheeze that I do actually need to breathe. That I may consider myself exempt from all other biology, but even I can't escape breathing.

Last night I went to a restaurant to say farewell to a very, very close friend who is leaving to travel for six months. I'd had dinner at home beforehand in an attempt to a) save money and b) not eat very much. She went and ordered a big plate of something for me anyway, and I would have felt ungracious if I hadn't eaten it. The problem was, it brought on a panic attack in the middle of the restaurant. My heart was almost thumping out of my chest. So I vomited in the restaurant bathroom to calm myself. I'm not proud of it. In fact, I feel worse.

It's a lovely day today. I woke up to a garden washed in the soft gray of a cloudy morning. Beautiful.

· · ·

I had the appointment with my psychiatrist today.

Waiting in that little musty waiting room that reeks of anorexia, another girl walked in. Pale, delicate. Space underneath her jeans. Flat eyes.

I was called in. I cried a bit, talked a bit. Just wanted to get out.

My psychiatrist is thinking of changing or upping my medication. Apparently I may be becoming "immune" to my current dose, which would explain the prevalence of blackness lately.

I got myself home. I walked and caught a bus, I guess. I can't actually remember.

I have to be honest. I feel awful if I'm not. I could just not say anything. But then how could you trust me? And how could I trust myself?

I had a major binge before the appointment because I was so nervous. *Major.* A couple of kilograms of food. I was in pain. I felt utterly ill. I purged in the shower. The most comprehensive, enormous purge I have ever done. I know I should feel ashamed of myself for being such a hypocrite, but I'm not. I'm just proud of myself for getting it out of me. I don't have any weight leeway anymore. It's not like when I was –kilos lighter and could afford to keep binges in. I can't now. I'm *normal.*

I keep reliving the feeling as waves of food rolled up. I am ashamed to admit that it was really satisfying. To the point where I almost didn't want to stop. I only stopped when I hit some pear, because I realized that purging fruit was just so *dumb.*

I guess…it took on a bit of a conceptual meaning for me, today. I ate to fill some intense dissatisfaction and purged to rid myself of all the swollen emotions I swallowed with the rice and baked beans and bread and walnuts.

I don't know. I'm sorry. Tomorrow will be better.

• • •

I am supposed to meet up with that guy this afternoon. I'm not feeling too nervous right now. I woke up to a message from J and A on MySpace and two messages from this lovely London poet I've just "met" over the vacuumed wasteland of cyberspace, so I am feeling pretty good.

I'm now scoffing a whole packet of Special K. But who cares. I don't right now, to be honest.

It's lovely and sunny. Bum bum bum ba ba ababa ba ba bum bum …

• • •

So now I'm so nervous about meeting this guy, I'll probably throw up unintentionally. That'll be new for me.

I've never done this "date" thing before. This is the first test of this new "self" I've been trying to piece together, and I am, quite frankly, utterly terrified. I have never felt so anxious in my life. How the fuck am I going to get out the front door?

This is going to take some serious act-engineering.

. . .

Let's start from the very beginning...a very good place to start.

Lucy, literally shaking with nerves, stands outside the appointed cafe and tries to listen to some buoyant music in an attempt to hold herself together. She is convinced it was all a joke and he will not show up. She then starts to relax a little, because she knows he won't turn up; in fact it's almost certain. Starts actually listening to her music (The Strokes) and watching the people around her.

He shows up. Ah shit. There's that smile. Her knees start shaking involuntarily. From this point...it's all a bit of a blur. Let's see. They talked at a little table for two hours.

They just talked and talked. Lucy felt perfectly comfortable telling him about last year. He was also introverted and shy at school. He also "found" himself at university. He also hates fake people.

Lucy was completely herself. *And he liked that.* When they were saying goodbye he repeated how glad he was he had given Lucy his number. They talked about that "connection" you immediately feel with someone. It's taking everything Lucy has to sit at the computer and write this down. Ideally she'd be running and jumping around squealing.

They hugged. *Lucy* kissed him on the cheek.

And then...? A text message. Ten minutes after they'd left each other:

"Lucy, you've overwhelmed me with happiness. I know I said this already, but I'm so glad that I gave you my number."

Excuse Lucy while she screams and spasms crazily. She needs to catch her breath.

Perhaps she just imagined it? No. That message is actually there.

. . .

Oh dear, I feel quite lightheaded. I have no appetite whatsoever.

And this, of course, had to happen the day before my exams start.

I'm feeling somewhat *distracted?*

At 11:12 a.m. I receive the first text message: *"Why oh why can't I stop thinking about you?"* I was, at this time, sipping a soy mocha and attempting to do some group study with friends. I read it and couldn't breathe. My chest hurt. I actually felt winded. Perhaps it was a joke?

I responded with: *"I could say the same... I could hardly sleep last night for thinking of you. I was convinced I'd imagined everything."*

Then a bit later I sent him another one: *"I love the rain. I'm very...distracted. I wish this philosophy exam would disappear in a puff of purple smoke. Gah..."*

At 1:57 p.m. he responded with: *"I love the rain too, but when I'm indoors. Wish I was at home in bed."*

At 2:20 p.m. he wrote: *"I know this may sound very obsessive and I really don't want to scare you away, but I really can't wait to see you again."* I read this just as I was walking out the university gates. It was cold and gray. A little "Oh!" wedged itself in my throat. Again I felt breathless.

I just can't help thinking that maybe it's all some sort of joke. This would have to be the first guy in the whole history of Lucy-existence to have ever taken more than a fleeting interest in me.

I accidentally forgot to take my brain to university today, though. It has taken to disappearing lately. It will probably turn up early tomorrow morning, and I'll have to spend all day sticking it back together in time for tomorrow's English exam.

I went to my philosophy exam; tried to write and couldn't. My inability to answer the questions sent me smashing downward again. I shakingly handed it in before time and ducked out.

I crept home in silence, feeling utterly despondent. Firstly, my iPod's battery failed, and the city just isn't the same without Sigur Rós; and secondly, I was stressing over seeing him again. Somehow he's made me out to be more...I don't know. More than I am. And now I'm scared of disappointing him. Ahh. I just texted him to tell him that I work tomorrow night and no one ever comes into the shop...and he just texted back with *"Well, I might just have to pop in."* Again I felt little funny heart twitters.

I don't like feeling emotionally...twittery. It makes me feel weak.

I didn't even realize I had only had half a coffee for dinner yesterday until I stepped on the scales this morning and had lost a little. It really is so easy, isn't it?

. . .

It's raining. I'm at home alone. I am not hungry. I desperately feel the need to write...but can't. I feel the need to create something...but I can't.

I have a cold. I feel empty and purposeless. Perhaps I will fiddle with my book. Or continue standing in front of the heater in my undies. I've been managing to stay at –kilograms for some time. –kilograms. Yes. This is the next stage. I managed at –kilograms for about six months. And before then...I'll not dwell on it. Time was of no consideration back then. What I'm trying to get to, in a roundabout way, is that I can accept this. Last night I could, even if I can't right now.

There's a time when you decide you just can't be bothered dedicating your life to self-destruction anymore. And there's got to be a time when I decide to stop reminiscing about my near-achieved self-destruction. Just because my brain blanked out that year doesn't give me leave to romanticize it. For it was anything but. You know that.

The garden is frozen in a kind of psychological sympathy. Sullen clouds, rain balancing on brown leaves, bare branches glistening. And the "wheep" of a bird. Always a bird. Always a sound to splinter the silence. Lucky, I suppose. Or I might have just ebbed away into that funky gray.

. . .

I stood in line at the Arts faculty office to ask for my exam special consideration form. It was very hushed. A whisper of paper. A sigh.

And then? *Crrrrunch.*

Pause.

Crrrrunch.

Slowly, deliberately.

Crrrrunch.

It was beyond infuriating. I just wanted to whip around, see who it was who was doing all the "crrrrunching," and say, "For fuck's sake, won't you shut your fucking *crrrrrunching* up?"

However, I didn't. I turned discreetly and glared at the offender while she stuck her nose in a poster advertising some seminar for such-and-such. Everything about her irritated me. From the ridiculous hot-pink striped poncho to her short hair and middle-aged-ness. What was she doing *crrrrrunching* up Sydney Uni? What the hell was her problem?

Jesus.

I turned back around and focused my annoyance on the chunky man in front. He lope-danced out and breathed heavily.

Then I noticed the mature student who flounced around with her sleek, little black backpack and her enrollment forms, and a look in her eye that whimpered: *Oh yes. I am at uni-vers-ity. I am a mat-ure stu-dent. I have authority. Mmm, hmm. Oh yes. Now back off, or I'll beat you around your young heads with my extensive pen collection. Uh huh.*

I almost ran out of that goddamn office, did run down past the lawns, out the front gates, across the road, to the bus stop, hopped onto a city-bound bus, did the ticket-thing…and was accosted by a short, squat, balding old Greek woman brandishing "Who is Jesus?" pamphlets. I grimaced, but refrained mightily from shouting "Fuuuuuck! Get out of my face!"

Chugged down Parramatta Road, stupidly hopped into a shop, was ambushed by two little twittering sales-girls. Twitter, twitter, flounce, bop. *Leave me fucking alone and stop your goddamn twittering, or I will throw your coat hangers around.*

Finally, almost there…Wynyard…a bus to home…thank God…there it is…

Ahh FUCK. Not her. An old acquaintance. Lovely! Little twisted smile. I beam plastic lips. I sit next to her, as is polite. Make polite chitchat when I'd really rather be silent and stick my eyes to the window. Chitter chatter. Giggle. Sigh. Chitter chatter. Giggle. Sigh.

I got home eventually. Then I binged and felt annoyed. Then I had an early shower, which necessitated a stupid purge but nevertheless calmed me down.

Now I am studying and feeling sorry for myself for being so short-tempered. Sporadically laughing at myself. Pulling my hair out. My lips are dry, my throat is sore, and I'm getting another goddamn head cold.

But I can be irritable if I want. So there.

* * *

Someone made my bed this morning. Which really irritates me. *I* make my bed. And they found the slip of paper P gave me with his mobile number on it, which I keep under my pillow.

I'm seeing him tonight. I think.

I hope.

I'm nervous.

* * *

I am an idiot. I don't know what's wrong with me.

I stumbled home and just wished, *wished*, for someone to either murder me on the spot or run me over.

I'm still here, obviously.

I am such a fucking, *fucking* idiot. I might as well starve myself into bones…and not stop.

Language actually can't express how much I loathe myself at the moment. No…it's not even loathing. I just want to throw myself off a cliff and have it all taken care of. Have it all end. I just want to get rid of me. I am the most pathetic waste of space.

What the fuck is so wrong with me? What. The. Fuck. Is. So. Wrong. With. Me?

This is it. I'm sick of it. I'm sick of everything.

There aren't any cliffs around here.

I just don't know what to do. I just don't know what to do.

I just don't know what to do with me.

I'm trying not to think too much. Otherwise I might just do something.

I have no words to describe myself.

I wonder what would happen if I just took all of my pills. Like that. What would happen? Can you overdose on antidepressants? I'd probably go barmy. More so than now, I mean.

I am floored with despair. I can hardly blink, let alone type. I'm sorry. I'm going to go away now.

Untitled
Voiceless,
Something stretched taut between us.

The streetlights are sick.
Plugging my eyes with pallid yellow,
At least I can't see yours.

You go.
I knew you would.

This dark footpath is smeared with smiles.
I step on their lips
And give them cold tears.

• • •

They're changing my medication.

Sleepless night. Argument with Mum over me not wanting to talk to her about my relationships. *Last time I checked, it was my private life, thanks.*

I don't know. It's silly. P triggered it off. It all seemed to be going so well. And then, I don't know. Something failed. I failed. He just became indifferent. Told me his car was "too dirty" to offer me a lift home. So I walked home, by myself, in the dark. Felt utterly despondent. Walked slowly, slowly, leaving parts of me along the way.

I got home, sat in my pitch-black room for a few hours. Scrabbled out that half-poem *Untitled*…lay in bed sleepless; restless; eyes open; tensed.

It's just hard coming to terms with your own inadequacy. I've been aware of it, for a long time. But being whacked in the face with it is a shock every time.

• • •

Why? What happened? I just feel so lonely.

Damn.

Maybe I should send him a text message apologizing for whatever I did, or did not, do.

Let's watch me fall flat on my face again.

"Okay, now it's my turn to be obsessive. Something seemed amiss when we said goodbye the other night…we might as well be completely honest with each other. Is something up?"

No reply.

I guess I could have realistically expected him to reply within six hours if he was going to reply.

I feel pretty low.

How on earth did I stuff this one up?

Going from telling me that I make him "overwhelmingly happy" to ignoring me? In the space of three days? We saw a movie—that's all. Is there something I'm supposed to do movie-date-etiquette-wise that I missed out on?

Is "So, do you want to see a movie tomorrow night" date-code for "So let's have sex in the back row," and I failed to initiate or comply?

I just don't get it.

What is wrong with this guy? Or more to the point, what is wrong with me? Any other girl would have fucking climbed on top of him in that goddamn movie. Ahh, sorry…but that's just not me. And there was an entire row of preteens near us.

I mean, *Jesus.*

Or maybe something's up, and he has no credit? Or maybe he's lost his phone? Or maybe I sent the messages to someone else? Or maybe they got lost along the way? Maybe, maybe, maybe, stop-fucking-excusing-this-fucking-obvious-brush-off-and-start-hatching-a-plan-to-get-to-London-and-snag-this-poet-you're-cyber-flirting-with.

"Fuck P, I'm inexperienced in this and it's agonizing. If you're trying to brush me off, can you at least tell me? You know me enough to know I don't play games."

• • •

I'm sitting, jiggling and fluttering, with my eyes on the keyboard and peripheral vision on my mobile…just waiting for the screen to light up and for P to tell me to stop being such a twit and that he's actually falling hopelessly in love with me and was scared of it himself. Good God I'm young and stupid and silly.

I feel curiously liberated. I'm not going to let guys fuck around with me. If he can't deal with honesty and girls who aren't in the habit of flinging their vaginas and hands around the place, I'll keep looking until I find someone who will. It's just a shame the one I have in mind lives on the other side of the world and, in this case, is eight years older than me.

I have to have a shower; stand aimlessly wasting water this dry country does not have while I will my body to make itself clean with no effort. Then I must do some sit-ups and frolic about my room.

By that time I'll be all ready to start feeling sorry for myself again. So I'll peep at my phone, see no message, and hit myself over the head a few times. Then I will listen to melancholic music and cry in bed to make my life feel more dramatic before finally falling into sleep and dreaming about kiwi fruit like I did last night.

● ● ●

I'm tired. My self-esteem is teetering on the edge of "just acceptable" and is threatening to fall again. Tumble, really.

I went in to university this morning to hand my special consideration forms in for my exams. It was cool. The sandstone of the quad was laced with the distilled blue of winter sun and all the leaves had fallen from the creeper straddling the front entrance. It was quiet. There were very few people. My little shoes rasped over the pavement. The grass was very green and the flimsy veil of morning mist was persisting despite the hour.

Later, I waited to hand my last form in at the English department office. It was unattended, so I leant against the yellowed walls and breathed that musty institutional smell. There was an honors lecture in the room behind me. "Milton and Rhetorical Discourse," the schedule said. I listened in a sort of stupor to the effusive self-involved pomp of the speaker. Ran my fingers down the plastered wall. Watched the brown doors. Tried not to bristle as a gaggle of schoolgirl visitors chattered through the silence. I pondered the door to the disabled toilet. It had a handle much closer to the ground and a strange strip of metal around the bottom of the door.

Everything was very still. A scholarly stasis.

I manage it back into the city, where I am supposed to meet up with a friend, and confuse myself over buses and which side of the road I should be on. Disorient myself and ring home. In a mental muddle, I jump on a bus and fervently hope it will take me to where I need to get.

I wander around a dusty and very sterile interchange for a while. Finally find the friend I was to meet up with, albeit almost an hour late. We walk along the cliffs from Bondi to Coogee. I try not to let my self-criticism take hold. *Fuck Lucy, say something! You're so fucking boring, she'll be regretting she ever met up with you. Be more colorful; she hangs out with colorful people all the time, and you're so tedious in comparison. Yeah, why not stretch that silence out a bit more and really look like a socially challenged loser? Oh yes. Of course. The alternative is saying something so predictably inane that you'll wish you'd stayed silent. Idiot.*

I had roasted eggplant, pumpkin, artichoke, and bocconcini on toasted sourdough with pesto. And our water jug came with mint sprigs and lemon and lime slices. I sweated over whether to order the "risotto with gorgonzola, baby spinach, and roasted pumpkin, with optional walnuts" instead. Prohibition scratched in chalk.

By the time we had finished, the day was tiring. Retreating into the peach stretch of late afternoon that just inspires hopeless nostalgia. I try to avoid going out at that time, generally. It depresses me. I can't work out why. I don't like the daytime anyway. Why do I get so emotionally caught up in its slow fade into dark? Perhaps it is the end of the day signaling the imminent coming of another one…or the feelings associated with one more day crossed off; nothing achieved save a (failed) outing with a friend.

In one big step, I took the train from Bondi to Martin Place. I have a train phobia. I just don't like them. But I managed it. Even if my hands were white from gripping my bag the entire way. Even if I was certain of imminent destruction below Kings Cross. Even if I just *knew* that the shady guys a few plastic rows behind me were planning said imminent destruction. And of course, we were always about to crash; always about to run off the rails; always about to sideswipe the oncoming train; always about to be blown up by some ill-timed-peak-hour-destined backpack.

I did get home eventually, though. Stumbled halfway on sore feet and asked Mum very quietly if she'd mind picking me up at the War

Memorial. Charged in, washed hands, skulled water, grabbed apple, threw work jumper on, checked for keys, ran out, got to work.

And of course the Internet had to have failed. I spent the hours of my shift eating cough tablets (tasty) and playing Minesweeper on the computer. It was deadly. Deadly boring. Deadly in the real sense in that I was just about ready to skewer myself with a coat hanger. Or pummel a mannequin. Or take the lovely large orange-handled scissors to one of the evening gowns. Such a satisfying snnnip, it would have made. Snip. Snnnnip. Snnip.

I am not feeling good about myself. My mood really has plunged. Even over the course of me writing this. I feel utterly dejected. *Dejected.* Rejected, too. The dejection stems from my feeling of self-inadequacy; the rejection stems from the social equivalent.

Flimsy, flaccid, and flat. All in one. The personification of boredom. She's coming to a dumb stupor near you.

(Claps weakly.)

• • •

It would seem that P was too good for little me. I never have much luck with this because:

- *I don't play games.*

- *I don't play hard to get if I like someone—I mean, that's just dumb.*

- *I think too much for some people's comfort.*

- *I don't sexually throw myself at guys.*

So…they don't know what to do with me. Except to, in this case, speed off indifferently in their car and leave me to walk home in the dark by myself.

There goes my confidence. Whoomph.

But its collapse has been somewhat tempered these past few weeks by this boy in London. Argh, Internet romances. I flinch away from the keys, just typing that. The stereotype seems so constructed; so desperate. But I'm actually being serious. I don't think it is unreciprocated, and I don't think it is imagined. It feels very real. Sort of discomforting to my sensibilities. But hey, it's a bit of fun, yeah?

To: Lucy
From: L

I hope you don't lie awake all night. Do you think
you can get to know someone like this? I have spoken
to others on MySpace...but not really like we are?
Hmmm.

You know what. Feel free to find this odd, I kind of
wish you lived in England, then I could put a voice
and flesh on your words.

You really are very beautiful by the way...

xxx

• • •

My brain is on slow-motion overdrive. It won't shut up, but won't
process anything either. So I'm left staring witlessly at the screen,
willing words but failing sense.

I stepped home to the bleeding of the streetlights and slow
blackening of the trees. Silhouetted against a mauve sky; restless in
the wind.

I can't remember what I thought of. I can only remember how
the wind tightened my cheeks and rubbed my lips dry, and how my
head seemed to float over my guttered shadow. Stepping in the gate
of home, it felt like I had lived a hundred lives since locking the shop
door fifteen minutes earlier.

The wooden arch near the gate had been blown down in the
wind. I stepped over a decapitated climbing rose and blinked at the
yellow of the outside light. Stood for a moment and watched the sky
shutter black.

Inside, I got my apple juice, gnawed on a sourdough roll.

Went upstairs.

Sat where I am sitting now.

Contemplated a month-old doodle on a piece of paper tagged
"Burma" in scrawling black felt tip.

Now I am very calmly deflated and get a hot little sting when I
think of P, damn it. Am I so desperate to be loved that my feelings
fly and bloom and crack and blacken within weeks of themselves?

From the crashing around downstairs, I'd say Rose the cat has
brought another poor sewer rat in.

To: Lucy
From: L

You are five foot nine. (I have only just noticed.)
That is taller than I imagined...which kind of makes
you more beautiful, and now I have to reimagine you
naked dancing on the bed in your socks...blimey that's
amazing. Ha, ha...

xx

• • •

And sometimes...

Somewhere in among the music of Sigur Rós and sweet, clipped grass and wooden bench; somewhere next to the creamed Greek yogurt and scuffed black ballet slipper and at some indiscriminate distance from the musked hair and eyelashes...

The earth reels and pulls you down; head to a hollow and eyes to the sky; to gape again, stupidly, at the whole of whatever it is that has come together (in some furtive piecing of edges or shyly knitted periphery). And in that moment, in that moment of time stretched from construct to (un)worth, you roll under the assurance of that-which-was into same-time immensity and irrelevance.

Only to bury your cheeks in the grass, converse with ticklish ants, and laugh with the awkwardness of knowing nothing and everything at the same time.

• • •

Slowly, slowly, slowly, but very, very surely...falling in love again? Oh God.

To: L
From: Me

When we meet up (in Venice? in London?) we can
make crumbs together. I am wonderful at shedding
crumbs. I was just nibbling on some dark chocolate,
and my desk is already strewn with little chocolatey
shards...I figure it's like slurping. I mean, you can't
really enjoy a big, thick slice of wholemeal toast
with cherry jam unless you spill some crumbs. Or in
my case...lots of crumbs. Non-crumb-spilling and quiet-
sipping-rather-than-slurping are just two irritating

constructs of politeness designed to dull my gastro-
nomic enjoyment.

I'm finding it difficult to stop thinking about you.

xxx

• • •

I went to get some toilet paper and a glass of apple juice.

Down the stairs, curl around the bend; step, step, step. Kitchen.
Parents washing up.

Lounge room. Brother watching *Whose Line Is It Anyway?* and
laughing into his headphones.

Dining room, no light. I step carefully on the floorboards into the
darkened hall to flick the light switch. The front door is open, the
screen door crisscrossing the streetlight.

Apple juice in hand, I lean my forehead against its fine screen.
The twilight breeze curls to burrow between my shoulder blades,
the leaves of the magnolia nod. Overhead, a dark sky pink-pricked;
stars shying from the city lights.

And I tried to remember when I had last done *this*.

Perhaps it had been a decade…more…since I stood at the front
door similarly one half-lit night before Christmas. Years and years
ago. For no reason other than to listen to the world settle down to
sleep. To watch the streetlights pop, the birds hide under wing, and
the city shutter to a blinking close. Just conscious of the entirety of
everything and the extraordinary peacefulness.

I didn't turn the light on.

Finished my apple juice, though.

To: Lucy
From: L

Crumby sheets. Dusty notebooks. Big king-size
bed...Hanging baskets. Clammy limbs and the Sunday
Times.

You are wonderful.

I am wishing that:

a) you lived in London so I could see you after
   work

b) that I wasn't running out of words to describe how much I like you. When you visit this stinky city

You won't be shy around me.

We have shared intimacy

with letters and full stops.

Kiss (one day I hope for a real one).

. . .

Lonely and disheartened. Just for a little. Those boned thoughts are shuddering behind my eyes. But I am "living" now. That is worth it.

Right?

I think I'll just skip my shower and slide into bed next to my dog. I'll have him sleep with me tonight.

I feel uncertain. I've poised in my tiptoeing contemplation of this new light. Just enough to feel the drag of the shadows behind me. And everything's stupid. And inarticulate. I can feel it, but I feel ashamed to word it.

All this "recovery" feels so meaningless. A desperate plugging of time.

And I feel transparent again. Flimsy. Disengaged. Not only monochrome...but indistinct.

```
To: You
From: Me
```

I sometimes get this little jostling ball of frustrated energy in the pit of my stomach, and all I want to do is throw myself around wildly and scream. Just SCREAM incoherent words and tunes...and wave my arms and legs around until I collapse with the sheer exhaustion of being myself.

You're bringing on that feeling a lot, lately.

I need to have a shower. But I'll make it quick.

xxxx (all of a sudden these kisses don't seem quite as innocent...heh!)

To: Lucy
From: L

Don't worry about the kisses. Here are some less than
innocent ones in return.

xxxx

· · ·

She was too young.

Little jeans wrapped around wasted thigh. A little, green blouse.
Short sleeves with barely an arm showing through.

Very white skin. Black hair. I looked at her for too long, and she
saw me. I shrank back into the bus shelter, willing my arms to fade
back to then, willing my legs to part and crawl away into space.

She turned. A little face, round. Peaked. Bagged eyes. That very
particular look, that very particular glint of petted panic only recog-
nizable to those who have been there.

I watched a fat pigeon tiptoe along a window ledge.

Flossed and glossed, the heeled and vapid clapped past in twos.

The midday sun cut my eyes against the glass.

And I thought: *Well then. How about it?*

I slapped my neck where a loose hair was pretending to be a
bug.

*Again? Just to make sure I can do it properly? Just to prove I can do it
again? And go further? Surrender more?*

I contemplated dinner. I contemplated the sweet apple juice and
stodgy banana bread I'd had for lunch. I contemplated the Toblerone,
the yogurt.

I remembered the blankness and the gray, the nothing, the all,
the cold and sufficiency. I remembered how easy it was to go that
way and how hard it was to come back. To regain any measure of self
after such a sacrifice.

But...perhaps not. Perhaps not, now.

I'll put the idea away for another day's instability.

It's too hot and I specially saved nachos for dinner. And besides,
not only am I going to save the world, I am going to *write it*. And then
I will go to Mongolia. Scooter around Eastern Europe, give myself
some romantic disease, adopt street cats, upend those legal twats
and snip their wigs. And then I will have outrageous affairs with

men and women in multiple countries and time zones, give myself completely, write my soul in pieces, ride a Jersey cow in a field of the Western Front, paint humanity, and eat black sticky pudding until I turn into a coconut.

My iPod has died. I am getting a new one for the same price as fixing the old one. And on the back I will get a little engraving:

Au coin silencieux
les ombres lisent

which means "In the quiet corner the shadows are reading." And...perhaps they are.

```
To: Lucy
From: L

Morning darling. I hope that you are all comfy and
messy in your sheets.

KISS and a cuddle and perhaps one more kiss on your
nose and one more on your soft lips that I imagine
a lot when I should be doing other things, my love.

xxx
```

· · ·

I finished university at twelve o'clock today, so I could crawl home early. Two-hour torts seminar involving offbeat scenarios as to whether A could be charged if s/he were stung in the eye by a bee while driving and then swerved onto the pavement and hit B. I said that A should have kept her window up as it was foreseeable something could fly in. My tutor laughed and said I'd make a good lawyer.

I was so tired this morning I had to sneak out in a break and grab another coffee to zing myself up. It didn't work and I spent the last hour nodding and blinking sluggishly as half of me dozed and the other half desperately tried to look fascinated by corrective versus distributive justice.

But really, it is fascinating. Very dry, very formulaic, but fascinating. I love it. I can't imagine anything worse than being a lawyer...and I'm only doing it in view of working for the UN and humanitarian justice, but I'm really enjoying it. I like things that make me indignantly angry. There are so many areas and concepts that need reforming. And I never realized before just how much "law" is a philosophy, as opposed to a practice.

My new iPod gave out halfway through the Kinks on the way home which annoyed me greatly. Awkwardly sat next to a girl I used to go to school with on the bus and tried to make polite, socially acceptable conversation, failing for the most part, but hopefully I'll never see her again. She was so loud…she always had been. Cringingly. No wonder no one else was talking on the bus. They were all listening to her sex-romp tales. One of those insecure girls who swears loudly in the locker room and looks around to make sure she caught some attention.

Everything is bizarre. Those little moments when our mortality hits us in the face; on the bus to university this morning, we lurched really sharply as some woman in her red car swept in front of us and abruptly braked. All the people on the bus were thrown against each other and a hissed "*Shiiit*" broke out…and it was peculiar because as soon as we realized our limbs were all still attached and our little bubbles hadn't been grazed, the fat man sitting in front of me went back to digging around in his ears, the orange woman to my left went back to her music and hair-twiddling, and the permed and puckered lady beside me returned to the tut-tutting and examination of her gloves. And I sat there feeling strangely overwhelmed. I scrawled in my little book:

> *We staggered forward sharply; and in that second the naive*
> *hush broke. The fragility and innate mortality of ourselves, the*
> *transience and terrifying instability of existence, gasped. Another*
> *second and polite distance descended again.*

Back to our inane newspaper poking and forehead stroking. False reality alarm. I just sat there and felt curiously frightened. Swallowed the nonchalance around me with wonder.

To: You
From: Me

My love,

After falling out of bed and eating too much muesli,
I tripped up the stairs to find your message. It made
me smile...and shiver.

I dream about the world. I dream about the sheer size
and breadth of it, the intense variety of culture
and history and life stretched across its surface. It
makes my head ache. Thinking about the universe makes
my head ache. As does thinking about the roll of mil-
lennia. The billions of people and animals scrambling
around with their own little spheres of existence...you
over in London, me down here in Sydney. My head aches
a lot. And I get so frustrated with the enormity of
it all I could scream. In a happy sort of agony, I
suppose.

I need to touch you. I know what you mean: it's not
as though what we have is "un-real" but more that it
isn't concretely substantiated. I don't know. I just
need to hold you. Mentally, I think we're already
together, but I need you beneath my fingers.

And I did indeed stretch most gloriously this morning.
Arched and long. And then I closed my eyes and
breathed very softly and tried to imagine you next
to me.

It is overcast today. The trees are naked and very
still.

I have to clean the windows. I have to pack for my
trip to Canberra. I have to have little psychological
conversations with the sleeping you. I have to avoid
the muesli. I have to try not to distract myself too
intensely with thoughts of your hair and your breath
and your skin.

To: Lucy
From: L

I keep checking my inbox for the next Lucy message like a deranged old man waiting for his "Readers Digest"...and when it comes I get smiley and happy and I reply and then the whole process repeats itself like a merry-go-round but without the music or the wooden horses.

This is for you. And everyone who waits:

Your fragile head in a scarf, your crisp white wrists in my hands, barefoot and fenced in by lisianthus.

Pink blooming hearts and heads and red lips splay wide, soaking up the closeness of the breathless day

as the sky turns slate burnt blue and lavender. Dark wads of space filling up with a restless weight. Look

here in four months, the little blue boats that hunker on the lake will be removed and stacked in a bunker

one on top of the other, locked in kisses at the bow breathing creosote. No need for you now Mr. Pedelo.

I saw the flash of the sky before it reached my ears, a second a mile. Bowling along it will find me here

soon, slacken with my indelicate feet tickling the lawn, open chest and wilting. The sound is how they warn

you, rolling like a truck heaving load over a parched hot tarmac. Gust blows the top off the lake and calmed

little blue hulls laugh in the shadow of a wallowing song, I count the passing seconds until the crack and flare come.

In the Rose Garden it is still gentle, even though clouds are blackening quickly, the fresh wheeze does not shout for me. In four months, or less, I would show this small piece of turf, its fresh parting where lain I have built all

manner of fancy, observed the bend and sway of novice bark. Your rain wet mouth and twinning arms, a slice

of my internal reel. The first drop collapses on breastbone, only one second apart the spark almost touches crescendo.

No, Lucy. A carrot and salsa does not constitute dinner.

Fine, then. I'll go and cut myself a pear.

I am lonely.

I am feeling flattened again. Actually, that is wrong. I don't feel *flattened*, I feel *flat*.

I need another word.

dull   drab   lacklustre   toneless   glossless   blunt   reticent inarticulate...*pappy*

I just realized I spend endless hours on the Internet in a desperate attempt to avoid thinking. It's just too hard and too sharp and...discordant.

• • •

L makes my heart twinge bizarrely. It's probably lucky he's on the other side of the world, or I'd be blitheringly in love with him. I'm doing a good job of it at the moment, anyway. Mum refuses to let me go to London, point-blank. I argued and argued, but I just kept hitting brick walls. I mean, logically it is ridiculous. I know that. So we're going to meet up in Zurich. In November. I will rent a little room near the Old Town, and we can just talk and talk and talk. And I can hold him. And he can give me the little kisses he sends me via e-mail, in person.

At university we've been talking about depression as a Western disease, a disease of modernity. There has been a loss of idealism in the world. A loss of innocence in the Western world, especially. Whether you can attribute this to the breakdown in religious or communal ties; or the commercialization of industry and the individual; or the "scientification" of the world and experience as we know it... I don't know. But there is a weariness. There's a hole in the collective psyche.

I think that's behind a lot of the psychological disorders burgeoning today. This loss of identity and of purpose. Whether we realize it or not, society has "grown up"...and grows more disillusioned the more it tries to explain itself. The more we explore the void that is life—because ultimately, isn't all of this meaningless? —the more we lose of ourselves. Or at least that which once kept us grounded and compliant.

In the shower, feeling the steam press on my skin and the hot water flood over my back, I felt that very familiar little stab of doubt. I had it with J and I had it with P. Multiple times. Chronically. Disbelief in the sincerity of anyone claiming to like me for who I am. That familiar feeling of withdrawal; the familiar thought pattern: *Don't be ridiculous, you silly girl. He doesn't like you. This is the INTERNET. Stop before you get hurt.*

The idea that for me, all is a waiting act…a suspended Godotian reality, with me, tight-lipped and breathless, fearfully awaiting the moment the smiles become a parody. The moment when the dull core is laid naked; wrapped clumsily in a polka-dotted ideal.

But he keeps coming back.

• • •

I'm constantly cranking open that little trap door to anorexia, just to look quizzically (nostalgically) at the staircase leading to the darkness underneath.

It is so heavy, and my arms will ache. But it is harder to close than it is to open.

I feel as though I'm wheeling through cycles, creaking open the door, hovering, succumbing to the first stair, the second, before hauling myself out and creaking it closed again with all the energy I have.

It's draining because one way *is just so goddamn easy.* Just lift the latch and stumble-hop downwards. Easy.

It's just the coming up…or the half-hearted attempt to keep the door closed altogether. That's what's hard.

Life is hard and there's nothing romantic about shying away from it. There is nothing to rationalize a retreat, in this respect. *You retreat, you die.* You surrender. You. Give. Up.

Anorexia is giving up.

It is giving up on this screaming challenge: LIFE.

I don't do that.

I fight. And if that means cementing that trap door over…

At least then I won't be stuck in this hopping cabaret of opening-and-closing and going-up-and-down.

I can always put a nice potted plant on top. Just to remind me of what lies beneath. And of the life above.

To: L
From: Lucy

Wow...excuse my lack of vocab...

It is now twenty minutes since we hung up and you
went back to bed, and I sat there all kind of dumb
and mute and lost for words and excited.

I loved your accent. I thought actually that it was
incredibly sexy, and your laugh was stunning. I'm
so glad you phoned. I was shaky afterwards. It is
bonkers isn't it?

I like that you ground me. I have been feeling really
anxious about it because I don't really know what
to do about you, as in where to file you. I worry
intently that we will disappoint each other and that
all this is an illusion. So there we have it. I get
up early on a Sunday to e-mail you...even though I
haven't met you.

• • •

Oh dear. I want to hold him so much I can almost feel me aching...This
is complicated and inconvenient and stomach flipping. Damn.

• • •

My psychiatrist told me one thing at my last appointment that I will
probably never forget.

"Lucy," she said, *"an eating disorder and depression was the best thing
that could happen to you. In fact, it's the best thing to happen to anyone."*

Pause.

"It gives you the rare opportunity to discover yourself."

I sat.

I digested.

I understood.

So all of this is meaningless; we are insignificant; life is absurd
and short-lived; humanity is mired in its own despair.

I ponder the idea of "life" frequently.

The things that keep me going are the tiny, the minute, breath-
taking in their beauty. The perfection of a flower. The wind in the
trees. Stars at night. Luxuriating in sunlight in the morning. The
little trail of ants marching through the grass. Apparently meerkats

teach their young the same way we do, in "classrooms." All infinitely meaningless, but important.

It places us in the overall scheme of things. It is good to know this, and to keep our own inferiority in mind.

It is not good to let ourselves be drowned by it.

Because ultimately this life is all we have. As meaningless, as agony-ridden, as deeply ridiculous as it is, we have nothing else.

So why throw it away? Why not take some small pleasure in a little blossom shyly hovering to the ground?

This is your chance to rediscover yourself.

What a waste of time if you fritter it away.

• • •

L sent me a very drunk-sounding e-mail message this morning. We had a very intense multiple-hour conversation again last night.

I read the message, my heart pressing on my lungs. And replied with:

To: L
From: Me

Darling,

So far I've been sitting here for fifteen minutes trying to work out what to say. This is one of those times when words seem inappropriate, and I'd much prefer to just take you into my arms and kiss that silly head of yours.

The truth is I wonder if YOU are real. I miss YOU. And it's bizarre. And discomforting, because it makes me feel weak.

And I wish to God you weren't on the other side of the world. I'd much prefer to be torturously in love with you and be able to see you than held off at a distance like this.

You could not "squash" me. You stimulate me. That is the end of the matter. As for feeling guilty and frustrated...I can understand the frustration, but the guilt? Guilty for what? Silly age gaps? "Leading me astray"? (Ha, I snorted typing that. What a load of shit.)

I don't want to ignore you, and no, you are not full of shit. And...I hate me too, so you're not alone in that. Except I'm coming to realize that the people who hate themselves have the least reason out of everybody. It seems as though as soon as someone is given a brain to think deeply with and an emotionally sensitive core, they end up hating themselves. Which, I think, is a reflection on society, not them.

I love your honesty.

All we can do is see what happens.

Love, totter home and tuck yourself into bed. Think of me. I'm sending a soft goodnight kiss. We'll work something out.

Damn this. Damn him for being so wonderful. Damn my sentimental temperament. Damn our similarities and the fact that I think we've fallen for each other. Damn the fact we met over MySpace. Damn all of that. It's fucking infuriating. The truth of it is, he is putting his soul on display for me, and I am doing the same. This isn't pure unbridled lust like it was with J. This isn't the need for comforting validation like it was with P. This is one of those people I just want to be with. I just want to listen to. I just want to look at. I just want to touch.

• • •

I saw A yesterday. Not only was I on time, but I had actually planned to take her somewhere; as opposed to our general Hyde Park ramble. We shared sun-dried tomatoes, artichokes, mozzarella, and pesto on toasted Turkish bread and laughed over the irony. We both had cappuccinos. We talked and rambled and scared the waitress and the people sitting next to us. We ogled a nut shop. *Full* of fucking nuts. Cinnamon almonds. Buttered macadamias. Peanut brittle. Fucking cashews coated in chocolate.

We bought almonds in dark chocolate and giggled.

Ate them subversively in a bookshop while I tried to find something for A to read. I couldn't get past the existentialist authors ...

We frolicked and laughed like maniacs.

I am going to Zurich with L. This is quite definite. For seven days. I've found the most glorious little hotel in the Old Town. We're going to go to all the art galleries, collude poetically, eat pastries, walk through the cobbled streets, sleep, laze in front of the heater, and frequent the antique bookshops.

I feel disconnected this morning. I haven't been weighing myself because it was too depressing. I was surprised when I hopped onto the scales this morning and found I'd lost weight. This would be amusing if it weren't so dangerous.

• • •

I have had the most extraordinary binge…it feels like it will burst from my distended stomach…walnut coffee sticky buns (which I cooked), the toffee that indirectly appeared alongside, cereal, toasted walnuts…

It actually feels like it's eating through my stomach wall when I bend over.

I
WILL
NOT
PURGE.

You see? I'm not fucking purging. And to prove it, I'm going to have a shower and put myself in the situation that makes purging easiest—and I won't do it.

It is such a waste of time. (And I've lost weight anyway.)

I am so sore. So swollen. This is disgusting. I'm going to start crying soon. *It is so uncomfortable and I feel so nauseated.*

Damn this. I quite simply *haven't got* another few years of my life to give away to self-destruction. I want to save the world, remember?

• • •

I didn't purge. I went to bed and lay awake for hours. Slept fitfully.

The food in my stomach pressed on my back all night.

In the dark, I was acutely conscious of all the little movements of my body: the little jerks and twinges from my left ear down to my little toe on my right foot. In the delirious post-midnight hush, I thought I could feel the food leaching out of my stomach to collect in globules under my skin. I fearfully ran my hands over my stomach, my breasts, the tops of my thighs. Nothing. I almost laughed at myself. *How ridiculous.*

And darkness being the enemy of rational thought, I seriously considered the possibility of the food squeezing my heart and lungs and leaving me to die. Breathless and bloated.

Again, I almost laughed out loud at the part of me that was genuinely terrified.

I slept and woke sweating profusely; I slept and woke freezing; I slept and woke to the rumbled purring of my fat cat sitting on my feet; I slept and woke to my head thudding into the wall; I slept and woke to intense nausea; to a thought that I would actually need to vomit for sickness—then spent the next half hour deciding where I would be sick if I actually was.

I will not weigh myself. I have just finished a scrabbled-together breakfast of tomato and a poached egg and some yogurt and a coffee…I seriously think I will not be able to eat any carbohydrates today. Just thinking about them makes me retch.

Work today.

• • •

There was a letter for me in the mail today. A comfortingly square envelope: acceptably white, my name and address blackly scrawled. *Par Avion.* Royal Mail.

I left it for while. Left it to nap on my desk. Anticipated. Ran my finger slowly over the inked words, the sticky-tape. Opened, the matted sheen of a pebble fell from its hold. And a poem:

Black Pebble
A silent rebellion, this act, stood here
with a limited capacity for hedonistic folly.
Lasting as long as it does until my wallet
runs dry and I am pulled back from her.

On a glimmering marble bar, polished
and smooth and cold to touch, I stretch out
my bitten hands, home manicured; a habit not
dropped despite the application of mustard.

There were many, but I chose you due
to your size. You will not be missed,

the hole which you left when departed
can quickly be filled by pushing another few

in from each side. They may be larger, look
impressive with their sheen dark skin,
but they hold no recollection.
Expensive rocks for decoration's sake.

A little black teardrop nimbly slid within
my shallow pocket, quietly wrapped in excited
skin. Thumbing you dull, I rubbed
my little act into your smooth face. Imprinting

this plot, ready for your next journey, cello-taped
onto black scrawled cream paper as evidence.
Quite unexpected, dim, and used, once
cleft from your sleep, you lay in her delicate hand.

I slipped it under my pillow. Where P's number had been. Where
J's number had been, for the first few searing weeks. Where my tears
have rested; where diaries have slept; books hurriedly concealed at a
footstep of a parent. Sitting at my desk, I can feel it there. Between
the sheets. Tangible; real.

• • •

It is disconcerting when mottled vomit stares back up at you from
the bathroom drain.

Especially when it stares up at you two days after you purged
your self and confidence into the clean enamel of the hand basin in
one hot heave.

• • •

Slept fitfully in the newly settled heat. My legs sweated trails through
their moisturizer and glued my calves; my hair clung to my neck.
I had bizarre dreams about giant biscuits (with a lack of chocolate
chips) and ginger loaf (made with too much butter). I awoke ill; sick
with the very real feeling of having eaten. Lay there in the half dark
and contemplated throwing up just in case. Twitched my curtain

open to the blush of the sky and slipped my fingers under my pillow to close around the pebble.

I laughed into my other palm.

Don't be utterly ridiculous, Lucy. Turn over, cuddle your side, and go back to sleep.

• • •

Today was good, I think. Cold though, and I was impractically dressed. I stood in the rain and caught a cold. I had a nice salad and cheese sandwich. I held a functional conversation with a group of people, despite my shyness. (I think) I wrote a poem (I haven't looked at it again so can't be sure). I went to all my lectures.

Oh! And the marker of my history essay draft said that it was a load of "try-hard twaddle." She said it was "too literary," "too edgy"; that I was trying to be too clever; that I shouldn't use fragmented sentences; that I was literarily "pretentious."

I was absolutely indignant. Apparently she wants a nice, clean, pedestrian, boring, flat essay. How one can be dispassionate and conventional when writing about Virginia Woolf and the status of women in interwar Britain, I don't know.

But fine. I'll give her one.

On second thought…maybe I am just a load of try-hard twaddle.

• • •

The Chardonnay comedown, I presume.

I am lonely, I think.

It was my eighteenth birthday today. Oh joy. Marvelous. Bars, pool, Newtown, Lebanese, tennis balls, Chardonnay, Lindt chocolate, naan bread stuffed with coconut and almond. One engraved signet ring, some music for the soul, a cookbook purely of gourmet cupcakes, an IOU for a nice set of lead pencils from the Art Gallery of NSW, *Lolita* (Nabokov) and *Nausea* (Sartre). Plans for imminent societal initiation into the cult of the adult.

It hailed last night. Heavily. The only thing I thought of in my clinging semi-consciousness was "I think the air might break." Note to self: rain means very little when moderately inebriated, in good company, and warbling hymns to the geese of Victoria Park. Something…is not quite right between me and L.

…like "like minded friends," he said (or rather, typed).

The nails of my right hand cut into my lips.

Of course. Oh silly girl, practicality before sentimentality, always. Especially when dealing in hemispheres.

> To: L
> From: Lucy
>
> Thank you for the honesty. I knew something was wrong. You seemed distant, unconcerned. I was hurt and suspected as much.
>
> Maybe you are right. You're more grounded than me, so you must be. I have to learn and I am too young.
>
> We will need to speak about Zurich, considering we've booked flights.
>
> I am sorry.

• • •

I suspect I just tripped over my own nonsense. But please, please, tell me I wasn't just the cyber-fuck entertainment while he scouted around for someone better.

Am I really that…disposable?

• • •

I eat.

I bring it up.

I walked around university, sat on a bench, and cried.

• • •

Again, a fumbling for time. Time to heal, to smoothen.

J is back from overseas. The sky is clouded. Today I bought a little striped dress with big black buttons.

Last night I fell asleep to thoughts of fresh-cut grass and the little mushrooms straggling between the stones in a friend's garden.

I will be okay.
I need to learn that I am...sufficient.
Just
as
me.

• • •

Day of bemoaning on the front lawns with a close friend.

Mourning the lack of unstable philosophical boys with whom to take over the world and instigate personal greatness.

After scouting around and failing in our quest, we walked for two hours up and down Newtown. I saw a yellow polka-dotted skirt that would be mine now, were I not in such a hungry, depressed mood as I was then.

On another note, I hate bumping into girls at university who see you before you can avoid them and who insist on coming over, kissing you, and squealing, *"Lucyyyy! How arrrre you?"* Firstly, I hardly know you—so don't kiss me; secondly, you are not my friend—so don't kiss me; thirdly, that is an invasion of my precious bodily space—so don't kiss me; fourthly, I know how I am, thanks; fifthly, fuck off now—and don't kiss me!

I hug my delicious friends but don't really feel the need to recreationally hug every other female on campus. And now guys are getting in on the act. And they are notoriously bad huggers (unless poets, philosophers, or metrosexually inclined). I am quite good at distracting myself. Goes hand in hand with procrastination. I am sad, but I'd hardly know it!

• • •

Two possibilities:

1.   *I am actually putting on weight and turning into a flob.*

2.   *I am losing weight and flobbing my perception.*

3.   *I am maintaining my weight and I am finally seeing myself for my flobbiness.*

4. *I am maintaining my weight and tricking myself into feelings of flobbation due to stress.*

Yeah, so that's more than two possibilities. High five to all you smarties who worked that one out.

But to the crux of the issue:

ARGH. I AM A FLOB.

I didn't imagine the relationship between L and me. I have been reading over our emails. "Something" was very there until it choked on a reality. One reality, but a reality nonetheless.

• • •

I sat squat on the sandstone for an hour, waiting for A. Rain plopping at my umbrella, I stretched my legs out to feel the rain on my blistered toes and calves. Watched everyone running about like lame chickens. Finally caught by A, we went to a cafe and had wine (Chardonnay) and quesadillas with kumera chips (fantastic). I had a hot chocolate (ahh). Embarked on a grand city search for expensive chocolate. Finally settled on David Jones, from where I later ate a walnut-shaped chocolate filled with walnut and macadamia praline. A had a peppermint and dark chocolate snail.

• • •

That's what everything's about, right? *Not giving up.* And to a certain extent, *letting go of what has been to make space for what will be.* Living in the past is to live a dead life.

• • •

Coming home from work in the dark, I had one of those profound moments when I feel here-and-not-here; where I remind myself of the enormity of life and existence in comparison to little transitory Me...the spool of history; of times past and yet to come; Me as Me and You as You—singular, individual, yet utterly unremarkable. In this quicksand of thought, I stared at a streetlight for an age trying to work out the right word to describe the way the light traveled through the air. Too mellow to "cut," too spherical to "weep." Too puffed to "ooze" or "drip." "Waft" is overused. Perhaps streetlights can "smile"?

I stepped over the shadows slouching on the pavement and let myself melt into the navy blue of the sky. The streets were bare; the sky vast. The sharp city lights bled through distance. Passing beneath the brown leaves cuddling another streetlight, I forgot to systematically check the size of my thigh's shadow. I doubled back…but sloppily. An empty gesture. Of habit? Reminiscence? Of cult respect to a memory?

Perhaps this is it.
Perhaps this is it?

THE LIGHT?

In which Lucy finally looks up
and out, and picks some flowers

Perhaps.

While spring-cleaning my brain, I coughed up one green tablet, half a poem, carrots with mustard, and Lady Lazarus. So I naturally knitted them all together with a delightful combination of string and hair, and formed this book: a dimly sparkling transcript of my brain and "The Wondrous Adventures of Lucy," speckled with uncalled-for brain bits.

You've read most of it.

This is my attempt to show you how it is possible to breathe again. How it is possible to smile and laugh again. How it is possible to move on, but only with the understanding that the way is pitted with uncertainty and fear.

Giving up any comfort blanket is hard. I am going to be "eating disordered" for some time. It's still just as much a security blanket as it ever was. I'm just finding new, fluffier security blankets that don't secretly choke me when I'm not looking.

Anorexia is deceitful. It lies.

I can see through the lies now because I'm no longer dependent on them.

You're not sick enough to merit getting better, you say? You will never consider yourself "sick enough" until you're dead, and even then I bet most anorexics think they could outdo that too, somehow.

Below is my fail-proof guide to slowly learning to love yourself (*testing in process*).

LUCY'S FAIL-PROOF GUIDE TO SLOWLY LEARNING TO LOVE YOURSELF

Write a List

1. *Force yourself to recognize the fact that you are you, and that is that.*

2. *Realize that you can't change point number 1.*

3. *Find something about yourself that you like (for example, I like poetry. I like that I like poetry. I like rain, too. I love that I like rain).*

4. *Write down a list of what you like, the music you like, the books you like, the people you admire, what you want to achieve. Refer to this when you lose yourself momentarily.*

5. *Surround yourself with people who love you and think the world of you (they do exist, regardless of whether or not you choose to see them).*

6. *Be patient.*

7. *Do little things you enjoy. (I read poetry. I watch the rain. I step in nice big puddles.)*

This list isn't exhaustive. It's being developed. So far it's been successful. I don't love myself, but I've come to accept myself. Yesterday I even liked myself for a while.

Depression actually taught me how to live properly. I had to stop focusing inward and start looking outside. Not at the big, impressive things (they're generally disappointing) but at the little (and very underestimated) things. A flower in a gutter. Sand between my toes. Beautiful clouds. Soft breezes. Hugs. Goose bumps of happiness. Even if I felt them for only one second.

I never paid any attention to them before. Now they are my life.

Those moments of *hope*, of beauty, mean everything. They keep me going. Treasure them, and squirrel them away in your memory. They're very precious. And yes: they do signal something very important. They're the real you poking out of that dark shell...the real you singing out for a few minutes.

See? You're still in there.

Make a Choice

No one can force you to do anything. You choose. You always choose. You can choose not to weigh yourself; you can choose to have a dash of milk in your coffee; you can choose to begin that furtive stumble toward the light.

Conversely, you can choose to remain behind. You can choose to cower. You can choose to starve, binge, abuse yourself. It is a compulsion, yes, but it is a compulsion that can be fixed. Patched up. Knitted anew into a healthier form.

Biologically, your body is desperate to survive. Biologically, our bodies are not predisposed to obesity. That is a modern phenomenon. You may have erased any appetite control you once had, but you can teach yourself again. Draw up a meal plan and stick to it. Something you feel you can achieve. For the first month of my "recovery," I just ate an extra apple a day. That's all. Then I started having one marshmallow for a morning tea, as well. That is a start. It's a step forward.

You need to teach yourself to trust you again. It takes time. A long time. Your body is very clever. It will fix itself. It will reinstate its appetite control. It will not let you balloon forever.

Look for Colors

Anyone else get late-night calls from drugged-out lesbians? Because I just did.

I answered the phone to hear a voice slurring and speaking in a really bizarre high-pitched accent:

"I thought you said you were coming to the shop tonight. For the party? You said you'd meet me here at eleven."

"*Umm, sorry? I think you might have the wrong number.*"

"No. I don't. You gave me your number today and said you'd come to my party at the shop."

"*Oh, did I? I'm sorry...I don't remember that. Who do you want to speak to?*"

"A girl. I can't remember her name. Well, can you come?"

"*Ahh, no. You see, I'm just getting ready for bed.*"

"Oh. I need drugs. This lesbian took my drugs [incoherent rant of some description, "sex" and "cars" mentioned] and I really need them back."

"*Aw, I'm really sorry about that. I'm sure you'll get them back eventually.*"

"No! I won't! Can you bring some around? [Adopts whining tone] I have my period."

"*Aw, that sucks. And I don't have any money at the moment, I'm afraid.*"

"Oh. Do you want to have sex?"

"*Oh, I'm not really in the mood for that right now. Sorry about that.*"

"Oh. [Sigh.] Are you a lesbian?"

"*Ahh, no. Sorry again.*"

She/he hangs up.

Oh dear. But I keep incidents like this in my memory. I chuckle over them occasionally. Another little colored light to add to my life experience. Small, tiny, inconsequential—yes. But special, in a bizarre way. Like the guy I saw today cycling down a main road in very short shorts (with a trail of cars behind him), singing some high falsetto rendition of a Jamiroquai song. Just another little something to keep.

Insanity

You are not insane, you are anorexic. You are not hopeless. This isn't *you*; this is the *anorexia*.

Your thoughts are not your own but the result of your eating disorder. It funnels and distills everything.

I had some very poisonous conversations with my anorexic demon. I could never catch a clear view of her because she was always partially obscured by some depressed fog. This isn't madness. It's the awful, mind-twanging nature of this disease you have got yourself into and are reluctant to part with.

One of my close friends described the brain screaming as similar in sound to one of those milk-frother-thingies on coffee machines. Grating, painful, insistent. It doesn't scream now. Sort of whimpers occasionally.

It will be okay. I can promise you this. You may think you're all alone and don't need to answer to anyone but yourself. But you're forgetting about me, here. I'm investing a lot of emotional energy in this book because I believe in this. How you react to this will also affect me.

So go pick the little bits of yourself up that flew off in the smashup and super-glue them back in place. That's an order. Oh, and while you're at it, go tell that toothy, self-destructive damsel in the full skirt to fuck off. Politely, of course.

Watch

Keep your eyes and senses open. Notice things. Observe people. Write. Think.

I write mostly at night. I like writing on buses, too. There's something strangely magical about transcribing little gems of thought onto a scrappy piece of paper while you're surrounded by boring businesspeople reading the finance section. It feels somewhat subversive. Try it. We need more literary minds.

Pills

Laxatives, diet pills, appetite suppressants, and any other little hard things that are not vitamins. Naughty pills. Throw them away now, now, now. Jump on them. Cast them off into a river with ceremony.

Laxatives remove water weight. Not fat. In fact, you know what? Even anorexia doesn't remove much fat. Instead, it wastes the muscle. People of a normal(ish) weight generally have a lower overall body-fat percentage than anorexia sufferers.

Appetite suppressants muck with your internal regulation even more. This is just boycotting yourself. Adding more stuffing to the stuffed-up-edness.

Lies

"You look so much nicer with a bit of color in your cheeks."

"Oh, you're looking so much better."

"You're smiling/laughing/singing again!"

Since when did any comments such as those, or any of their ilk, ever, ever denote fatness? I know the thought process. It stabbed me every time. Whenever someone said, "I'm so glad to see your rosy cheeks back," my blood would beat through my ears. And I would think, *Oh shit. I'm fat!*

No. You are just less pale.

People are remarkably simple. We say what we mean unless we're trying to be smart or deliberately exclude someone from grasping our meaning. Color is color. There's one picture I have of me from that time, showing pallid, yellow, and thinly stretched skin, darkening to a curious orange around my mouth. I looked sick. And then there is another photo from a few months later, with my face a little more pale pink. No doubt I was reeling from the comments, but I appeared just as thin as before.

Brain

The brain is the last to go and the last to come back. It holds on and struggles valiantly, but when it gives up, it gives up. And it takes a lot of coaxing to start it functioning properly again. When eating was torturous, I used to eat and then lie down on my bed and cradle my stomach, visualizing all the healthy nutrients sewing my mind back together and filling in the holes. That is good.

Don't expect your brain to work normally. Don't expect for it to work anytime soon. It takes a long time. Months and months. This is normal. What you are going through is "anorexically" normal. I went through it. Honestly. It all makes so much sense to me, because I've been able to look back and analyze the past clearly, when at the time I was certain I was insane.

Emotional Pain

I can relate to this pain. Eating at first was like a self-inflicted torture. Feelings and emotions reared up that had lain dormant for months and months and months. If not years. It is terrifying.

It's so easy to give up at this point. So easy. But it isn't the way to go. If you go back, *that* is giving up. If you give up on the idea of recovery, *that* is a weakness. Because recovery is a lot harder than maintaining an eating disorder ever was.

You've been trying to avoid life for way too long. If you can, and I know it will exhaust you, try to almost revel in this burst of feeling. It shows that you are alive. It's just your fucked-up, eating-disordered thinking that's struggling and kicking and screaming at you to stuff your face, purge, and further abuse yourself. Your pain shows how strong you are.

Talk to it. I had raging arguments. *Fuck off. Fucking fuck off and leave me alone.* When I was alone, I used some pretty awful language. I'd get to the point where I was rolling on the floor and pulling at my hair, crying incoherently, desperately trying to evict something from me, trying to get rid of some demon.

This is what you're doing. You must expel this demon.

You will get there. How your body and mind are reacting now is utterly natural. It's trying to jerk you back into that hole. Just when you got a foot up. It gets easier the more steps you take; the further you distance yourself from that screaming black.

You will get there. You don't know your own power. Test it out. You are winning for as long as you hold out against this.

It will not always feel like this. These are the awful, *awful* first pains.

Dead End

Recovery seems to be one long process of a few steps forward, stall, another step, stall, and so on. The very fact you're not getting anywhere is a step forward. *You're not going backward.*

If the idea of "recovery" is too overwhelming, realize that you don't have to go the whole way at the moment. You simply need to go to the point where you are not as sick and are feeling a little more positive. Aim for a quarter of the way, and hang on to that for as long as you feel you need to. Then climb up a bit more.

Shyness

Give yourself a break. You're reading the words of someone who was so chronically paralyzed by shyness, she sweated before giving her order to a waiter. She never danced around in her room because she was convinced the paintings were watching her. She has spent many hours hiding in public toilets, cringing from people, pushing people away. You're reading the soul of someone who could, at one time, barely leave the house for timidity. Who was plagued by embarrassment and self-scorn.

You cannot battle psychological impediments and knots until you are physically a little healthier. Your mind is not the slightest bit interested in whether or not you can converse with people without hyperventilating. Your mind is trying to keep your body alive. Not until your body is healthier can your mind start mending itself.

Perception

Your perception is a lie. As hard as that is to fathom.

I used to scream with frustration because I couldn't understand how what I saw in the mirror could be so different from what others saw.

Before our brain recognizes any image, it is moderated by our emotional center. Which explains why I always look thin when I feel good, and why I somehow manage to bulk up as soon as I start feeling down.

If you're convinced you're chubby, you will see yourself as such. Simple.

But it isn't true.

Anorexia is a psychological disease. Your mind is sick. Your perception is sick, twisted, perverted. You are sick. Shake your head at me in denial, laugh at me, that's okay. I did that too. You are either reading this because you relate in some way or because you're interested in understanding. For the former: you are sick. Weight is no indication of psychological illness. Anorexia is, first and foremost, a psychological disease that chooses to manifest itself physically. For the latter: please read. Please learn. Please sever some of those prejudices and talk to people about this.

Obsession

I was tortured every day by food. The mental debates I had every time I saw food; the endless counting of calories and excessive walks around the block to burn off that naughty apple. I was my own demon. It felt like something was living through me, like I had a growth in my head who shouted at me that I was fat and ugly and worthless and that I might as well die because no one would care anyway.

In the earliest stages of recovery, there is nothing except obsession. Obsession with food, obsession with mealtimes, obsession with calories, obsession with exercise, obsession with self-loathing, obsession with obsession.

Some hobbies that I slowly taught myself to indulge in and which helped me distance myself from my obsessions included:

- *Reading poetry.*

- *Planning exorbitant overseas trips.*

- *Trawling through second-hand bookshops.*

- *Walking in the late afternoon/early morning when the light is clean and beautiful.*

- *Writing—about anything. Stream of consciousness, prose, babble...*

- *Highlighting notes with pretty colored highlighters in an attempt to feel organized.*

- *Evicting everyone from the house; turning my music up; dancing crazily.*

- *Drawing. Just try it.*

- *Writing down all of the things I want to do in my life. I still have my list. Everything from wanting to pick blackberries on the side of the road to studying English literature at Oxford. Everything. This really helped me. I would look at it when I was really, really low, and it would offer me some hope. One prerequisite: these aspirations must have nothing to do with your eating disorder.*

- *Fiddling with crosswords. These take up a remarkable amount of time and help whip that brain into shape.*

- *Listening to music.*

- *Walking to a park and sitting in the sun/shade; reading/pretending to read; watching the sky.*

- *Sleeping. This is underrated. Napping in the sun on a cold day is one of my chief pleasures. It feels so good, it could be sinful.*

- *Having bubble baths.*

- *Joining an online support community and getting to know everyone. The Internet forum I'm a member of has been a phenomenal help to me. I have made the dearest, dearest friends, all around the world.*

- *Singing loudly.*
- *Painting. Slapping and twirling brush cathartically. Voilà!*
- *Dreaming. Exorbitantly. Wantonly. Indulgently.*

Identity

The idea of your identity being caught up solely in the anorexia is one so familiar to me that I could shatter the computer screen in frustration. I *know*. But it is a lie, a very potent anorexic lie. It is wrong. You're talking to a girl who was utterly convinced that recovery would destroy anything she "had." You're talking to a girl who had no security in self; had no self, whatsoever. Who didn't know herself and used anorexia as a weak and ugly substitute. I wrote in my diary,

> I suppose anorexia was giving me a somebody to be...an identity of sorts when I couldn't find my own.

The thing is, *anorexia is strangling your "self."* This took me a long time to understand and to realize. It's the anorexia that is eroding your idea of self. It is only through the recovery of *your self* that you can reintroduce yourself to *you*. Carry on this way, *giving in* to the anorexia, and you can be sure it will kill any remnant of self you have left.

Failure

We have to change our perspective on "failure." Marya Hornbacher in *Wasted* writes: "It's hard to understand...that giving it up is stronger than holding on, that 'letting yourself go' could mean that you have succeeded rather than failed..."

The only "failure" I see is when we turn our backs on life and give in to the disorder.

I didn't used to think like that, though. It has taken time to realize that the true measure of *success* is the extent to which we embrace life. The extent to which we use our lives, not forfeit them.

. . .

So. What are you going to do first? I will not take "no" for an answer, okay? Death is defeatist, and you have far too much oomph in you for that. You're tired, yes, you're exhausted and spent and starving and sick, but it will only get worse if you let it continue like this.

I'm going to help you do this. It's always a difficult decision for me to make when I decide to involve myself with someone else's recovery. It's a very delicate psychological balance to deal with.

But I want to help. I refuse to let those torturous memories of the time I spent as a dispassioned bone sit there uselessly.

There is a way out. Furthermore, *you* are that way out.

Remember that depression is notorious for inspiring feelings of utter hopelessness and apathy. Have you talked with a doctor or a counselor? If not, you should look into it. I have no delusions; I would be dead now had I not sought and received medical help. In my case, zombification on antidepressants and gradual recovery was better than slashing my wrists or sticking my head in an oven.

Many people in our position are affected by inferiority complexes. I feel inferior to most people, for example. I'm constantly overawed by people, feel intimidated and not as important. So we're both there, okay? This is a "construct." It is a construct perpetuated by the disease to make you feel awful and worthless, and make it easier to starve and deny and abuse.

You need to realize that recovery from anything is a slow process. Especially from an eating disorder. I will tell you, it does get harder from here. But you are stronger than you think, even when you feel so weak. Grit your teeth; bear it. You have all the time you need. No one is rushing you. Take it slowly and at your own pace. *But have a pace. Don't expect everything to happen at once. It takes years.*

Escape won't happen overnight. You know this, but I'll remind you. Recovery and freedom from an eating disorder starts that moment you make one tiny decision: *that you will try.* Recovery is one long process of tiny decisions, little baby steps. A marshmallow. An apple. A dash of milk.

You also need to realize that you cannot see yourself objectively. I have said this previously. You have this view of yourself that is skewed by the self-destruction you've been indulging in for far too long.

Don't expect too much too quickly. Life doesn't all lighten and bloom at once, but don't give up on the idea entirely. It is slow. And learning to live again is much harder than continuing to give in to a disease.

It isn't a weakness. Living isn't a weakness. The race to self-destruction doesn't prove how strong you are. It just proves how reluctant you are to face life.

Emaciation is merely a stage in the duration of the illness. You give up and die, or you spend twice as long and twice as much energy crawling back to yourself.

We'll do this, okay?

• • •

So…now. I still have a prickly relationship with my body. Sometimes I like it, *like it*, with an edgily creeping excitement. Sometimes I don't. I still stand in front of the mirror and claw at myself in disgust. I have a "healthy" BMI of…or something. It may even be…now. I haven't weighed myself in a week and have been subversively enjoying a fruit bun or two. I can feel a fizzing anxiety, but I'm not going to let it govern me.

My arms are still thin, my collarbones and ribs still show. My stomach can be quite flat now it has acquainted itself with its natural function again. I don't get sore every time I sit down or feel that sharp spasm of pain at the base of my spine when I get up. It also doesn't protrude disgustingly through the skin. I can't span my upper thigh with my hands, just like I can't span my arms with one hand anymore. *Oh dear. I'm no longer eating myself.* But I can still hold on to my collarbones. My wrists still look delicate if I hold them like *this*. My feet don't hurt when I walk, and veins don't pop out of my arms and feet like they used to. I don't feel intensely depressed after food, and I don't sit on my bed unable to do anything but wait for the next meal. I don't compulsively run up and down the hall when everyone is out, and I have gagged that hissing mantra that tells me how worthless I am.

My thighs, today, are humungous. But I'm aware that that *could* be my perception. They were slimly toned yesterday, you see. Absurd? Utterly.

I battle with my alter-self every day. It presses me to believe I never had an issue, that I was never sick—or at least not sick *enough*. It is wrong. I'm on enough tablets for me to be paranoid about a) where they go, and b) the quantity of green and pink coloring subsequently ingested. Multiple antidepressants and sedatives. If I forget to take them, I have that all-too-familiar feeling of balancing on an emotional precipice...between hysterical laughter and a mind of black crayon. I didn't want to have to start taking them. I didn't want to be "helped." Those months of pill testing have no place in my memory. I have simply wiped them out. Once the sheer black dissipated, any happiness felt plastic. Sadness was extreme. Every emotion felt constructed and fake. Horribly pretend.

Anorexia has taught me much about myself and a lot more about the people I thought I knew...I can truly feel content and at peace occasionally, because I have great sadness and a splintered mind to compare it to. I'm even more empathetic than I used to be. I have my passions back. I spend my days reading, writing, and planning my future: a plan that doesn't revolve around what meals I'll cook when I finally get to London or the cheese I'll eat along the Champs Elysées. I am in an intense and *tangible* relationship with a wonderful boy and can now honestly say that I know what it is like to have a true heartache for someone—and not pretend. I listen to music again. I can actually laugh *and mean it*—and that is the most amazing feeling. I am not eternally constipated. I can eat most of what I like without stressing too much. I am weaning myself off the bingeing stage of recovery. I walk because I enjoy it, not because I know it must be done. I eat afternoon tea. I can read significantly more than a page a month.

Some days I string my brain along behind me like a helium balloon. Sometimes I drag myself along the gravel. But I am learning to love again. Not just other people, but myself included—arguably the most important.

What was I before? Dead. Metaphorically, of course. Although it could have been literal too. Easily.

But I "gave in" to the much harder choice of recovery.

And *life*.

NOTES

. . .

Page 6: *Of course, three years ago, I was your "average" anorectic.* Although "anorexic" is commonly used to both describe and label those afflicted with the disorder, "anorectic" is the correct noun, with "anorexic" correctly used in the adjectival sense.

. . .

Page 6: *In year 9, my English class studied* Stick Figure *by Lori Gottlieb.* Lori Gottlieb, *Stick Figure: A Diary of My Former Self* (Sydney: Hodder Headline, 2000).

. . .

Page 8: *My stomach felt strange when I thought of the exams, the HSC (Higher School Certificate).* The HSC is the highest and final award of the New South Wales educational system. It is awarded to students who have satisfactorily completed the final two years of school. The HSC is the basis for determining a student's UAI (University Admissions Index, a numerical measure between 0 and 100), which is then used to apply for admission into undergraduate study at universities or the like.

. . .

Page 11: *"Well, you certainly don't look anorexic."* Sally, Sue, or Susan later told me in my one (and only) follow-up appointment that she had said that as a "test" of my disordered thinking. Ah, yeah. More of an "excuse me, while I chuck you further and mercilessly into what I would otherwise profess to help you through."

• • •

Page 34: *Our future engineers, lawyers, sportswomen, politicians, teachers, mothers, gastroenterologists…you girls are sparkling with talent.* The guest speaker that night was an eminent female gastroenterologist.

• • •

Page 35: *"Strength doesn't always roar, sometimes strength is the quiet voice at the end of the day saying, 'I will try again tomorrow and never, ever, ever give up.'"* Mary Anne Radmacher said, "Courage doesn't always roar. Sometimes courage is the quiet voice at the end of the day saying, 'I will try again tomorrow.'" Somewhere in cyberspace I happened upon the slightly corrupted version first—which seems to me, in hindsight, a curious fusion of Radmacher and Winston Churchill.

• • •

Page 36: *Emotional Lucy flecked with anorexic sentiment.* Nostalgia to the point of willing relapse seems often to be part of a person's recovery from anorexia.

• • •

Page 46: *I met my friend A through an anorexia forum on the Internet.* I believe the media likes to label them "pro-ana sites." Some of them are, of course. Some of them revolve around the "thin is god" mantra. I used to be obsessed with them. I used to spend hours and hours of every day searching for them, sifting through site after site in an attempt to find one that would give me that subversive "rush." I was addicted to their sickening appeal. I felt part of something hidden and secret and dark. It was a dangerous time.

• • •

Page 60: *Reading* Wasted *last night, I had this deep, painful, irrepressible urge to go backwards.* Marya Hornbacher, *Wasted: A Memoir of Anorexia and Bulimia* (New York: HarperCollins, 1998).

• • •

Page 73: *Let's consider the newspaper article I read very recently, calling for normal-sized mannequins in shop windows.* Kelly Burke, "Keeping the Mould: Fashion Fights Anorexics' Charter," *Sydney Morning Herald*, January 26, 2007.

• • •

Page 74: *There is evidence that genes passed through families may predispose people to anorexia.* Tori DeAngelis, "A Genetic Link to Anorexia," *Monitor on Psychology* 33 (March 2002):34–36; Michael Strober, Roberta Freeman, Carlyn Lampert, Jane Diamond, and Walter Kaye, "Controlled Family Study of Anorexia Nervosa and Bulimia Nervosa: Evidence of Shared Liability and Transmission of Partial Syndromes," *The American Journal of Psychiatry* 157 (March 2000):393–401.

• • •

Page 98: *My "muse" and I met over the same "pro-ana" forum, at about the same time as I met A.* Sharon is a tremendously gifted painter, and it was on her idea and her initiation that the website We Bite Back was formed. She also wrote the foreword to this book.

• • •

Page 106: *I could never truly express why I developed anorexia until I read this in* Wasted. To be honest, I haven't opened that book again since I first read and annotated it. It was a very painful, and very triggering, read for me. As such, I can't give you a page number for this quote... It is one of the passages in the book that struck me with such truth; with such potent application to my own set of circumstances, that I suspect I'll carry it with me for the rest of my life.

RESOURCES

This is by no means an exhaustive list. It is meant as a starting point for your own research and initiative. Resources and support opportunities for eating disorders (for those suffering and their families or caregivers) are growing constantly. Internet sites have been listed, all of which have excellent resource and link pages (warning: many hours can be spent following endless, interesting, helpful, and relevant links!).

Academy for Eating Disorders (AED)
    www.aedweb.org/

Active Minds
    www.activeminds.org
    With campus chapters all around the country, Active Minds is working to engage students in conversing about mental health on campus.

Anxiety Disorders Association of America (ADAA)
    www.adaa.org

The Eating Disorder Foundation
    www.eatingdisorderfoundation.org

Eating Disorder Hope
    www.eatingdisorderhope.com

Eating Disorder Referral and Information Center
www.edreferral.com
Provides a searchable database of eating disorder treatment professionals and recent articles and research, and is updated every day. Also has an excellent resources section.

The Joy Project
www.joyproject.org

Mental Health America (formerly National Mental Health Association)
www.nmha.org

Multi-service Eating Disorders Association (MEDA)
www.medainc.org

National Association of Anorexia Nervosa and Associated Disorders (ANAD)
www.anad.org
or call 1-847-831-3438 for a help and referral hotline.

National Association for Males with Eating Disorders (NAMED)
www.namedinc.org
Many of the websites already listed have sections especially for men and boys suffering from an eating disorder.

National Eating Disorder Information Centre
www.nedic.ca/index.shtml
Fantastic resource library, listing articles, books, journals, videos, and websites.

National Eating Disorders Association (NEDA)
www.nationaleatingdisorders.org

National Institute of Mental Health
www.nimh.nih.gov/health/topics

S.A.F.E Alternatives
www.selfinjury.com
or call 1-800-DON'T CUT.

Something Fishy
www.something-fishy.org

We Bite Back (forum)
www.webiteback.com/forum

FOR FAMILIES AND CAREGIVERS

Families Empowered and Supporting Treatment of Eating Disorders
www.feast-ed.org
See particularly their excellent resources section for families and parents.

Around the Dinner Table (forum)
www.aroundthedinnertable.org
A forum for the parents of those suffering from an eating disorder.

TREATMENT CENTERS

Remuda Ranch
www.remudaranch.com
The website has a fantastic collection of articles.

Kartini Clinic
www.kartiniclinic.com/home
Specializes in the treatment of disordered eating in children and young adults, aged six to twenty-one.

The Renfrew Center
www.renfrewcenter.com

Lucy Howard-Taylor is a student studying English and law at Sydney University, a talented photographer, and a published poet. She has edited Australia's oldest literary journal, *Hermes*, as well as the university women's law journal, *Yemaya*. In between writing articles for the campus newspaper, she likes to eat cinnamon toast and dream about studying at Oxford. She lives in Sydney, Australia.

Foreword writer **Sharon Hodgson** is a freelance artist and the founder of We Bite Back, a web community created in response to pro-anorexia websites. She lives in Halifax, NS, Canada.

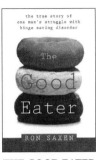